Rachel Mawston is uniquely qual   r-
sonal devotion for one primary re   w
more than ever; during times of s   ɹr
world, Rachel reminds us that the most important moments of our day
are spent in God's presence and in His Word. Both as her pastors and
friends, we have witnessed first-hand how God is using Rachel to help
people come into a deeper understanding of their daily walk with Jesus.
Be inspired and encouraged as you read.

Jon and Chantel Norman
Senior Pastors, Soul Church UK

Rachel Mawston is a conduit of godly wisdom. She gleaned so much
from the example of her parents before her and has in turn been a great
example to her daughters Melody and Mercy. The fact that Melody is a
co-author of these devotions says much about the transfer of wisdom
across the generations. Rachel has certainly dedicated her life to un-
earthing godly wisdom from the Word of God; she is ideally experienced
to now pass on some of that gold to you. Treasure it as you read it, and
live it as you learn it.

Steve and Joyce Dixon
Lead and State Pastors, Hillsong Church Brisbane

I am delighted to endorse this devotional. I believe it will equip and encourage you wherever you are on life's journey. I know and love both
Rachel and Melody – they have walked out what they have written, and
they would want you to read it while being willing to be challenged and
changed. I pray that you will be able to say: "It is well with my soul."

Margaret Stunt
Unlocking Ministries

Rachel and Melody write with vulnerability and openness. Their humility
and sensitivity draw you in to hear the voice of God for yourself. Mentoring comes in its various forms – this devotional is mentoring at its best!

Steve and Angie Campbell
Pastors, The C3 Church

Having known Rachel since we were children, I can testify to the fact that if anyone can help you give your soul a rest, it's her. Rachel cares about people, but she doesn't just leave it there. She cares about people flourishing in life, and as someone who has practised having a healthy soul over the years, I feel that there's no one better equipped to help us to do the same. Having her daughter Melody co-author this book makes it relevant to women of all ages and encourages them to keep their soul healthy in a world where everything screams the opposite. I know that by reading this book your soul will be refreshed and rested – you will be strengthened for your next season.

Louise Cherrie
Lead Pastor, Glow Church UK

Having known Rachel and Melody for many years, I am certain that the words in this book will leave you equipped and encouraged to live your life in an even greater way. I believe that their love for people and their desire to see those around them grow from strength to strength is what makes this more than just a devotional; it is an investment into your soul. It is with great joy and expectation that I recommend this beautiful work to you. It will be an incredible help and inspiration.

Lucinda Dooley
Lead Pastor, Hillsong Church Africa

Rachel lives a life rooted in the Word of God and led by the Holy Spirit. She gives her life to help others walk in truth and the freedom Christ gives through the Word of God. She leads by example and lives what she teaches; she is intentional and diligent with her own soul's health. We've watched Rachel not only help countless people, but also her own daughters Melody and Mercy in navigating the different seasons of life through staying anchored in the Word of God. Even when Melody was ten years old, she wrote messages based on scripture and would preach them to encourage her peers in kids' church. We know their insights will encourage and inspire you to help you find rest and restoration for your soul.

Brad and Karissa Kohring
State Creative Pastors, Hillsong Church Queensland

foreword by Bobbie Houston

Rachel Mawston
Co-authored by Melody Mawston

SOUL TIME

When your soul needs a holiday
A thirty day devotional

First printing 2021

Cataloguing – in – Publication data available

ISBN 978-1-9168912-0-3 (international trade paperback)

ISBN 978-1-9168912-1-0 (e-book)

Book Designer: Stuart Smith

With heartfelt appreciation for my parents, Trevor and Joyce Pimlott, and my late grandparents. Sedley and Mildred Pimlott, for the incredible legacy they have built over decades to prioritise and apply God's Word to their lives and their children's children.

I am thankful for the many nights my parents tucked me in bed, read a Bible story or scripture and prayed with me about whatever situation I was facing at the time.

Rachel

CONTENTS

The Lord is my shepherd, I lack nothing.
He makes me lie down in green pastures,
He leads me beside quiet waters,
He refreshes my soul.
PSALM 23:1-4 (NIV)

Understanding the mystery, wonder and challenge of the human soul is critical to wellbeing, strength, calling and destiny.

I came to personal salvation at the tender age of fifteen. I had no experience of the Word of God, its redemptive nature nor the reality that we are spiritual beings on a spiritual journey home.

So, to discover that our personhood consists of "body, soul and spirit" was not only exciting and illuminating — it became guiding perspective and truth that has enabled me to navigate the many twists and turns that accompany the seasons of life. When life screams chaos, or when the winds of adversity blow, there is a safe place in Jesus Christ, wherein our soul can find rest, repose and refreshing.

I have known Rachel for a number of years now. She and her husband, Steve, were part of our Hillsong College and pastoral team in Australia before returning to their homeland of the United Kingdom. She has always been a source of personal encouragement and joy. If I were to close my eyes, even now, and picture Rachel, I would see her beautiful smile, sparkling eyes and a Christlike countenance that exudes something special. What that tells me of her is that there is a well of salvation within that influences others.

Glance across the chapter titles of this devotional and you will see that she has a grip on life and has taken time to consider the many dynamics that can cause duress or challenge to the human soul. I personally believe that her own well of salvation can become a source of inspiration and hope for others.

Soul Time is a collection of devotions that will plant you within these truths. As twenty-first century culture and everyday life competes for attention, consider this a gifted invitation to press pause and reset your heart towards our wonderful Saviour.

With love,

Bobbie Houston
Co-Global Senior Pastor, Hillsong Church

INTRODUCTION:
WHEN YOUR SOUL NEEDS A HOLIDAY

Have you ever felt like you need a good holiday? Time to rest, replenish and recharge your soul?

Maybe right now you feel tired and depleted – that you've given out way more than your input. You long for some time out, rest, sunshine, a beach and a good book.

Holidays have always been a place of soul refreshing for me personally. I remember in 2007 when we were living in Australia and we had a stunning beach holiday in Noosa, Queensland:

I walk back from the beach to our hotel. Our daughters, Melody and Mercy, laugh and race each other, and my husband, Steve, cranks up the BBQ beside the resort pool. The sun shines, and the air is warm. The palm trees gently blow in the wind.

I feel rested, close to God, intimate with my family, and full of fresh vision for our future. I think to myself, "I wish I could bottle up this feeling to last throughout the entire year."

In that moment, I feel God speak to me. "Rachel, if you diligently take care of your soul, you can live this way."

What if your soul needs a holiday?

What if you could regularly take time to rest, replenish and recharge your soul? Maybe we can't physically go off on a holiday every time our soul feels depleted, but what if we apply holiday principles to our depleted souls, which enable us to flourish on the inside?

This is *Soul Time.*

Over the last few years, I have been on a journey of learning to regularly take the time to rest, replenish and recharge my soul. To ensure I am living out of a healthy soul and successfully balancing the demands of ministry, family and life – being more aware of what goes out from my soul and what goes into my soul. I am delighted to have the honour of sharing with you some of the things I have learned on this journey. My genuine prayer is that when you need *Soul Time*, this book will help you!

My eldest daughter, Melody, co-authored this book with me (here's a proud mum moment). She is currently aged 21 and is an amazing and talented worship leader in Hillsong Church Brisbane, where she is completing the last year of her theology degree and working on an album. We decided to write this together in the hope of connecting with a range of generations. Young adults (and older women) often ask me how they can make their devotional time with God more central and effective within the competing priorities and distractions of daily life. The essential ingredient to success is practically applying the Word of God. We hope that having both our perspectives will inspire you to prioritise your *Soul Time* and draw you closer to God.

I often find that a holiday is divided into three main sections. Rest, Replenish and Recharge. For me, at the start of a holiday,

I need to rest. To intentionally wind down. A chance to pause and reflect, to draw closer to God, and to identify those things going on inside that prevent rest. I then look to replenish. To intentionally refuel my soul with what I love (both practically and spiritually) that will cause me to flourish again. Finally, I need to recharge with some new ideas and dreams, a fresh impartation of direction from God's Word and confidence to move forward in calling and purpose. Melody and I believe that as you go on this three-part soul holiday with us, you will also be rested, replenished and recharged for all that is ahead.

Why not start this *Soul Time* devotional on your next holiday?

You can read it on your own, with a close friend, your mum, your daughter or another family member. We recommend you read it as a daily devotional, and take the time to answer the questions so that you can apply it to your own soul. After that, it can become a useful resource to which to refer – you can dip into a specific day that best describes your soul at that moment. We have created a "Delve Deeper" section for you at the end. Perhaps after you've read the daily devotion you may wish to delve deeper with scripture and additional personal or group reflection. Or you could do this section at the end as an "extended holiday" for your soul. You know what I mean – you've unwound, relaxed and recharged, but you just need a bit longer!

Whichever way you choose to read it – whether you are away on holiday or choose to relax back in a favourite chair in your living room – we pray that your soul will experience the rest and replenishment that comes from a good holiday. Now is the time to grab a cuppa, notebook and pen, and create your own *Soul Time*!

01. REST

PART ONE: REST

What's the first thing you want to do when you go on holiday?

Slow down and rest! Give your soul a holiday. Life may be hectic for you externally right now. Our prayer is that as you read this section, you will also find rest inwardly – rest for your soul.

"Come to Me, all you who labor and are heavy laden, and I will give you rest. Take My yoke upon you and learn from Me, for I am gentle and lowly in heart, and you will find rest for your souls. For My yoke is easy and My burden is light."

MATTHEW 11:28-30 NKJV

DAY 1: WHEN YOUR SOUL NEEDS TO BE HEALTHY

Beloved, I pray that you may prosper in all things and be in health, just as your soul prospers.

3 JOHN 1:2 NKJV

How healthy is your soul?

Today's verse is a special verse to me. I had the privilege of my grandparents and parents praying this verse over my life for decades. I have regularly prayed it over my own life and have "passed on the baton" by regularly praying it over my children's lives. It has impacted four generations of our family. As I write, we have a family of 62 (just on my dad's side) all serving God. Our family has certainly prospered in health by staying close to the principles in God's Word. I often write this scripture as a birthday greeting for friends and family, and today, I am writing and praying it over you.

John, the apostle who wrote this incredible verse, had the most beautiful relationship with and revelation of Jesus. He knew the value of a healthy soul. The soul is a collective of our mind, will and emotions, making up the part of us that is both internal and eternal. It's specially created for connection with God.

John Ortberg's book, *Soul Keeping,* describes the soul as the "operating system of your life."[1]

At the start of this "soul holiday," as you begin to unwind, let me remind you that you are dearly beloved! The word for beloved in Greek is agapetos. It is translated as "beloved", "dearly beloved", or "well-beloved"! You are His beloved, His dearly beloved, His well-beloved!

The word *agapetos* comes from the Greek word *agape*. It refers to God's unconditional, undeserved, unearned love. He doesn't love you because you are good; He loves you because He is good. So right at the beginning of this soul holiday, rest in the fact that God passionately loves you without having to do anything to earn or deserve His love. You can relax into your hammock, sun lounger or your sofa, knowing you don't have to do anything to earn His love today! Just enjoy it!

1 John Ortberg, Soul Keeping: Caring for the most important part of you, Zondervan, Michigan, p.42

Theologians for years have chuckled at the fact that John described himself as "the one Jesus loved" (John 13:23). This tells us that John knew who he was. John knew how much Jesus loved Him. John understood how much Jesus loves everyone. Now he reminds us in today's verse that we are His beloved!

When you discover you are His beloved, His *agapetos*, then you discover who you are and this truth transforms your soul. An unhealthy soul will produce an unhappy life. A prosperous soul produces a flourishing life. Are you living out from a healthy, flourishing soul or from a struggling, stressed out soul?

The good news is when you know in your soul that you are His beloved, you prosper internally; you are empowered to cope with whatever you are facing externally. When your soul prospers, everything prospers.

Interestingly, the Greek word for prosper in this scripture is *eudoo*, loosely translated as "help on the road" or "to go further." Do you need some help along the road to go further? If COVID-19 taught us anything, it was that we have little control over what happens to us in life. It's not easy, but we can take responsibility for what happens in us. We can keep our operating centre – our soul – strong. When we prosper internally, this is outworked externally into every area of our lives.

The focus of this devotional is to help you learn the art of thriving internally. You can develop a healthy soul!

TODAY:

1. As you begin your soul holiday, how healthy is your own soul right now? Are there any things currently threatening the health of your soul?

....

....

2. Starting from today, declare this verse over your own life and pray it over your family. Which members of your family could you send it to as an encouragement?

....

....

PRAYER:

Lord God, I thank you that you want me to live a healthy and abundant life. I pray that through this devotional you will help me to build a healthy soul – mentally, spiritually and emotionally. I pray that I will understand what it means to be your beloved. Help me to understand in a deeper way the manner of your unconditional love for me. I pray that as I accept your love, I will prosper in all things and be in health, just as my soul prospers. I declare this over my life in Jesus' name, amen.

DAY 2. WHEN YOUR SOUL NEEDS TO FEEL WHOLE

Now may the God of peace Himself sanctify you COMPLETELY; and may your WHOLE spirit, soul, and body be preserved blameless at the coming of our Lord Jesus Christ. He who calls you is faithful, who also will do it.

1 THESSALONIANS 5:23-24 NKJV (EMPHASIS ADDED)

Have you ever felt like you are divided on the inside? Or that somehow there is something missing on the inside?

Day 2 of your *Soul Time* is a great time to assess how whole you are on the inside. Sometimes, in the busyness of life, we don't always see what's going on inside our souls.

In 2017, during a particularly tough time, I sought help from a psychologist friend. Our time together was valuable, and he encouraged me around the importance of "self-care." This included the importance of speaking openly and honestly about my feelings and frustrations. I had to learn to become more vulnerable and transparent. He also highlighted the need for me to be more intentional with rest and exercise. I'm grateful for his help and guidance and put many of his recommendations into practice.

I began to feel better, but it wasn't long before I realised that my soul continued to ache and somehow feel incomplete. I discovered that "soul-care" is as important as, if not more important than, "self-care." Especially if you want to move forward through seasons of pain or disappointment.

What is soul-care? During this season, I learned that it's possible to give too much thought and attention to our concerns and worries. This "soul-stress" can then affect the other areas of our lives, especially our physical wellbeing. I notice it in areas like increased back pain or I find it hard to sleep. Life can start to feel fragmented and disjointed, and we become aware that we are no longer experiencing wholeness and peace.

A dictionary definition of "whole" describes "a thing complete, undivided, free of wound or injury, restored."

I've learned that nothing and nobody can make me whole – not my wonderful husband or family, not a new home, job, or moving continents! Only God can do this for me. Thankfully, God understands and lovingly wants to restore a right balance, bring reassurance and give His perspective to every situation: "....and you are complete in Him, who is the head of all principality and power" (Colossians 2:10).

Do you feel you are living in His wholeness and completeness?

Thankfully, God understands us, even when we don't! He lovingly wants to restore us.

We can easily be distracted from the One in whom we find our completeness. We are distracted by the constant demands of our family, our work or even the demands of our role in church. It requires incredible wisdom to juggle the multiple requirements that life makes of us.

The good news is that we can make wise choices, which bring us back to a position of wholeness in Him. However, this requires wisdom. James 1 encourages us to ask for wisdom and then believe that God gives it to us generously. However, James warns us of the danger of not trusting God completely (see James 1:7). When we doubt Him, we are described as being like a wave in the ocean. Then, in James 1:8, we read, "Such a person is double-minded and unstable in all they do."

James describes us a being double-minded and unstable. Hands up if you have ever felt unstable? However, the source of our instability is internal; it's the fact that we are double-minded. The word for double-minded in Greek is *dipsuchos*. *Dipsuchos* comes from *dis*, meaning two, and *psuche*, meaning soul. Therefore, if you are *dipsuchos*, you are two-souled or have a divided soul. When a person is unstable and inconsistent externally, it is because their soul is not whole.

A life that is whole begins in your soul.

Your wholeness and sense of completeness is only found in Him! It's "in Him" that you are complete. It's "in Him" that you are made whole. It's "in Him" that your whole being is satisfied.

One of my top five favourite quotes comes from Saint Augustine: "You have made us for yourself, and our hearts are restless, until they can find rest in you." God is faithful. Your soul can trust that He will do "it" in your life.

TODAY:

1. Identify the things that are distracting you from finding your wholeness and completeness in Him. What are the things that consistently threaten to divide you on the inside? Jot them down in your journal.

2. Who do you sometimes depend on to give you a sense of completeness? Imagine you find all your soul's wholeness and completeness in Jesus. How will this transform the way you live your life? You may wish to write these down.

....

....

PRAYER:

Lord Jesus, I know that I am complete in you. Help me to believe it from the very core of my being. I pray that today, you will fill my whole spirit, soul and body with your peace. Help me to live undivided and confident in the knowledge that with you, I am enough, and that you are faithful to complete your will in my life. In Jesus' name, amen.

DAY 3.
WHEN YOUR SOUL FEELS CLUTTERED

God, I invite your searching gaze into my heart. Examine me through and through; find out everything that may be hidden within me. Put me to the test and sift through all my anxious cares.

PSALM 139:23 TPT

Have you ever felt like having a good clear out?

Are you sick of looking at the mess and clutter all around your home?

Having a good clear out feels good, doesn't it? During a COVID-19 lockdown in England, we used the spare time to declutter our garage. It was a bit of a mess with all the stuff that we had brought back from Australia two years previously. After a couple of days of hard work, we were thrilled to discover that we had enough space for a cool hang-out area for Mercy and her friends. We built her a summer house. Some of the clutter wasn't necessarily rubbish; we simply didn't need it in this new season and location.

When we declutter our souls, we can create space for new thinking, plans and opportunities. We need to declutter old mindsets and disappointments that compete for the sacred spaces in our souls.

What clutter have you been storing in the sacred places of your soul?

Your soul holiday is the ideal time for you to ask God to help you sift through the storage rooms of your soul. Pay special attention to fearful mindsets, regrets, failures, loss or disappointments. Sometimes we place them in boxes, hoard them away in the dark corners, and they clutter and complicate our thinking and feeling. Sometimes, we would prefer to leave them in hiding as it's too painful to open old wounds. Why not invite a trusted friend or church leader to help you? Break open the garage door, and see whether you really need to continue hoarding these items. Are they of any real value to your future? Will they help you go where God has called you to go?

"For the overflow of what has been STORED in your heart will be seen by your fruit and will be heard in your words" (Luke 6:45 TPT emphasis added).

The scripture above says what is stored in our heart will be seen in our lives. The best way we can keep our hearts (our thinking and emotions) healthy, is to develop a lifestyle of regular decluttering.

Store treasure, not trash!

I used to work as a physiotherapist in cardiac rehabilitation. This involved helping people who had experienced a heart attack by removing internal "clutter" and preventing potential blockage of essential arteries. Most of my focus was on helping patients change their external habits (smoking, overeating, stress and a lack of exercise). By focussing patients on making these external lifestyle changes, it effectively prevented further internal clutter. The patients who diligently followed advice ended up enjoying a better quality of life than they experienced before their heart attack.

God wants you to have a quality life! What lifestyle changes do you need to make?

When you declutter the things stored in your heart and soul, it will be seen in the fruit of your life and the words you speak. Your heart is precious to God, and so are you – take the time to declutter your soul!

TODAY:

1. Ask God and a trusted friend to help you sift through the storage rooms of your soul, and highlight any anxieties, hurts or frustrations that may have built up over time that you need to get rid of.

2. Reflect on any words, worries, stress and offence that seek to settle in your soul. Purposefully give them to God now – let them go. Make sure you don't store them up. Just as your bin needs to be emptied and your dishwasher switched on and emptied daily, so does your soul!

....

....

PRAYER:

Lord Jesus, I thank you for your advice in your Word to keep my heart and soul free. I recognise I need to take responsibility to do this, but I'm asking for your help. Holy Spirit, help me to identify those things that are causing clutter, and give me the strength to let go once and for all. I will live free. In your name, amen.

DAY 4. WHEN YOUR SOUL FEELS FLAT

This is the day the LORD has made; We will rejoice and be glad in it.

PSALM 118:24 NKJV

Do you ever feel flat?

I've found that feeling flat can be harder to deal with than a meltdown. At least when you have a meltdown, you can have a good cry and hopefully reach out to others and to God.

When you feel flat, you just plod on; you don't always articulate how you feel. It's a silent subterranean sadness of the soul.

A couple of weeks ago, I was experiencing a silent low-level sadness. I just felt flat. While walking with a close friend, she told me she was experiencing the same thing! We were both functioning well on the outside – smiling, wearing our red lippy, doing our work, reading our Bible – but we both lacked energy and joy.

As we chatted, we recognised that feeling flat was due to a combination of factors. We were in the middle of the COVID-19 pandemic, and I hadn't seen my daughter Melody (who is still in Brisbane) for over a year. Mel couldn't come home for Christmas or be with us to celebrate her 21st birthday. I was missing being in church and hanging out with friends. I felt restricted and ripped off. My soul needed a holiday!

It's one thing to recognise that you are feeling flat and your joy levels are depleted, but how do you recover?

Joy is not necessarily a feeling; joy springs from a choice. Fifteen years ago, Pastor Bobbie Houston inspired me to walk and pray daily. I decided to declare the following every time I walked: "This is the day The Lord has made; I choose to be glad and rejoice in it."

The psalmist, David, wrote this when experiencing an intimidating external situation: "I called on the Lord in distress" (v.1), "All nations surrounded me" (v.10), "You pushed me violently" (v.13). Although distressed, intimidated and surrounded, David chooses not to be ruled by external circumstances but by his internal convictions. David starts and ends this Psalm with declarations of joy. There are declarations of praise woven throughout this Psalm. David knew the power of intentionally choosing to praise God because it lifts your soul.

When challenges surround you, on what do you choose to focus?

Jesus says, "In the world you will have tribulation: but be of good cheer; I have overcome the world" (see John 16:33).

Jesus never denied the reality that Christians will experience tribulation and challenging seasons. But He also instructed us to "be of good cheer." This seems counterintuitive! Why would we be of good cheer when we encounter tribulation?

Jesus teaches us not to focus on the challenges surrounding us but to focus on all He has done for us. "I have overcome the world."

Do you tend to focus on the first part (you will have tribulations) or the second half (I have overcome)? If you focus on the first part (life's tribulations), you can easily feel overwhelmed. If you focus on the second part (He has overcome), you will discover you too can overcome and find it easier to be of good cheer!

Often the litmus test of the condition of our soul is our level of joy.

Happiness and joy are different. It's often said that *happiness is external* and *joy is internal*. Happiness is about what "happens" to you. Therefore, happiness depends on external circumstances. However, joy is one of the fruits and evidence that the Holy Spirit is working *in you*. Therefore, joy is an *internal quality*.

I love Joyce Meyer's description of joy: "An internal calm delight" and "An unshakable stability."[3] A calm reassurance on the inside that all will be well as we delight in Him. Instead of a calm internal flatness, we can experience a calm delight! Our emotions aren't up and down; they are unshakable.

Joy is something we can internally activate each day by intentionally choosing it. Joy doesn't just happen. David said, "I will rejoice." It's a determination, a conviction, a choice to overcome what's happening around you and to stir up something within you – in your soul. Joy will lighten your internal load and help you have the "holiday feel" when you're not on holiday!

3   https://www.identitynetwork.net/apps/articles/default.asp?articleid=75458

TODAY:

1. Read the following Joy Statements and look up the accompanying verses. Copy them out on a pretty piece of paper or card, put it in a place where you will see it regularly and repeat them out loud!

- I have joy for my future (Proverbs 31:25)
- I have joy of my salvation (Psalm 51:12)
- I have joy that gives me strength (Nehemiah 8:10)
- Joy (laughter) is my medicine (Proverbs 17:22)
- I have joy in His presence (Psalm 16:11)
- I have joy in the Holy Spirit (Romans 15:17)
- Joy sets me above my companions (Psalm 45:6-7)

2. Go for a Soul Time walk today and say to yourself, "This is the day the Lord has made; I choose to be joy-filled in it." Overcome that flatness! Make it a daily choice

PRAYER:

Lord Jesus, your Word says you had joy more than your companions, even when you knew you were to endure the cross. May my day-to-day life be marked with joy regardless of my situation. I thank you that you already overcame for me so that I don't need to live overcome or flat. Today, I choose joy in Jesus' name! Amen.

DAY 5. WHEN YOUR SOUL IS FRETTING

Surely, I have calmed and quieted my soul; like a weaned child with his mother, like a weaned child is my soul within me [ceased from fretting].

PSALM 131:2 AMPC

Are you an overthinker?

Do you find so many thoughts and feelings competing for space in the real estate of your heart and mind? Do they grow increasingly louder when you're busy, creating internal anxiety, which causes you to fret?

One dictionary definition of fretting is "the action of wearing (or gnawing) away."

The worries of life can gradually erode and gnaw away at your soul. This reminds me of a very unwelcome guest in our first home as a married couple. Interestingly, it was in a village called Frettenham! We lived in a beautiful little country home. In the middle of winter, various rodents would pay us a visit. Usually, it was the little field mice. But there was one rodent we will never forget. We knew it wasn't just a mouse because it gnawed through a wire in our alarm system and woke us up in the middle of the night. Then we noticed it gnawed its way straight through a thick pine door to a cupboard situated underneath the stairs.

Steve will happily admit he is hopeless in some of these practical areas (sorry, darling), so we called in my Uncle Alan to come and help. Steve was standing in his dressing gown eating his Crunchy Nut Cornflakes and watching proceedings as Uncle Alan looked for the rodent. He opened the cupboard door and picked up a roll of carpet. This disturbed the invader, and a huge rat jumped up and ran straight over Steve's bare feet. It was dramatic.

When we finally caught the rat, we looked inside the carpet roll and there was a whole pile of Crunchy Nut Cornflakes! When we checked the box of cornflakes, sure enough, the rat had gnawed a hole in it. The rascal rodent had been taking the cornflakes from the box to his nest in the cupboard! Steve had been eating from the same box of cereal as the rat. As a result, he didn't eat Crunchy Nut Cornflakes for ten years!

Our worries and anxieties can gnaw away at our lives, and we don't notice it – until it builds up, and we feel a little frayed around the edges!

How do you handle this internal gnawing at your soul and "cease from fretting"?

I was blessed with two beautiful baby girls. Both slept through the night from about eight weeks old. But at around 16 weeks, my eldest daughter, Melody, started waking again. She was hungry, easily disturbed and upset. Fretful. I started supplementing her milk intake with some solids, which seemed to be what she needed, and it wasn't long before she was once again content, peaceful and not constantly looking for the next meal (although she has become quite the foodie in recent years).

In Bible times, people were familiar with high infant mortality rates. Therefore, they celebrated a child's weaning as a natural and important part of their culture. If a child reached the weaning stage, it greatly increased the likelihood of good health and longevity into adulthood. Weaning depicts the development from a passive dependence on the mother to active trust.

King David beautifully writes Psalm 131. He was a man of war, and he was being pursued by his enemies externally. Internally, he was being pursued by the anguish caused by some of his huge mistakes and personal loss. In his humility, he notes the vulnerability of a young child at rest with his mother. David observes that just like a child's contentment is being with his mum, true comfort and contentment is found in an intimate relationship to God.

There have been times in a busy season when just reading Psalm 131 brought calm to my fretful soul. I would picture a weaned child on its mother's lap, still close enough to be dependent on maternal provision but growing in maturity and trust that the next meal would come. A quiet confidence and contentment, a calm security and safety, with no more unsettled fretting or crying, knowing that all will be well.

When Melody and Mercy were very young and became unsettled, I would gently rhythmically tap their chest, as if calming their heart, and use hushed tones to settle them.

Even now, I often put my hand on my own heart or stomach and tell it to settle. I'm learning to "still my soul" when it starts to fret, when anxiety starts to gnaw at my soul (see Psalm 46:10 "Be still and know that I am God.").

Be still and know. Not "be still and believe" or "be still and hope it works out." "Be still and know that I am God."

God is the great I Am. God is with you, nourishing you. His hand is gently on your heart, whispering unconditional love, bringing safety and security in ANY circumstance. I love how Charles Spurgeon describes weanedness of the heart: "This sacred weanedness of heart is possible under any circumstances. It surrenders our desire to the safe keeping of our Heavenly Father."[4]

Today, make sure you surrender the desires of your soul to His safe keeping!

---

4   Charles Spurgeon, *The Complete Works of C.H. Spurgeon, Volume 21*, Delmarva Publication .Inc, Sermon 1210.

TODAY:

1. What little rodents have been gnawing away internally at your soul? Ask God to help you identify them, bring it into the open and remove them.

....

....

2. Picture yourself as a child on your heavenly Father's knee. Sense His hand of never-ending love gently tapping your chest and Him saying, "All will be well, my daughter."

PRAYER:

Heavenly Father, I ask that you would help me to learn the art of surrendering all the things that are gnawing at my soul. I surrender them to your safe keeping. You are the great I Am. I know that you are God. I trust you with all these concerns and surrender them to you right now. In Jesus' name, amen.

DAY 6: WHEN YOUR SOUL IS DISTRESSED

Love Melody xox

So then, my soul, why would you be depressed? Why would you sink into despair? Just keep hoping and waiting on God, your Savior. For no matter what, I will still sing with praise, for living before his face is my saving grace!

PSALM 42:4 TPT

Have you ever felt so helpless in a situation that you just didn't know what to do or where to turn? When you received that phone call of bad news, when a relationship didn't work out?

Maybe you have come on your soul holiday to recover after a challenging season in your own life.

There have been many times when my soul has been in distress and in need of replenishment. When we feel so anxious or disheartened about something, we can easily lose sight of the power of God's presence in our lives.

I was reminded of this a few years ago, shortly after my grandad passed away. It was halfway through our youth conference, and I was helping oversee the worship, when our family found out the news. I went home early that night, distressed and upset. Grandad lived in England, and we were living in Australia at the time. One minute I was leading worship and feeling full of joy at a youth conference, and then I felt waves of sadness crash down on my soul. I felt so far away, and I didn't get to say goodbye to him. As a teenager, I hadn't lost anyone in my family before, so I wasn't sure how to respond.

I was rostered to lead worship the next day, but nothing inside of me wanted to step onto the platform. At the same time, I knew I had committed to it, and another part of me felt I needed to do it. I remember driving to the camp that morning for rehearsal and bursting into tears as soon as I arrived. I started the worship set by reading Psalm 42:5-6 (TPT), which has now become my favourite passage of scripture:

So I speak over my heartbroken soul, "Take courage. Remember when you used to be right out front leading the procession of praise when the great crowd of worshipers gathered to go into the presence of the Lord? You shouted with joy as the sound of passionate celebration filled the air and the joyous multitude of lovers honored the festival of the Lord!"

It seemed as if these verses were written exactly for me in that situation, and it continues to remind me of the faithfulness of God. I felt God's peace and presence come over me during that worship set, and I knew my lovely grandad was in heaven worshipping with us just the same. My soul was downcast, but as I praised God and focussed on Him, I experienced a deep sense of awe and wonder for my God. That moment became one of the most memorable and most powerful God-encounters I have ever experienced.

My mum happened to be there that day, and she had her own encounter with God:

I walked into the building at Hillsong Mt. Gravatt, Brisbane that day feeling very downcast. At the time, I was probably unaware of how much Melody's grandad's death had impacted her heart. She had left home much earlier, and I slipped in at the back of the auditorium when the worship began. Towards the end of the worship, the lights were dimmed and Mel was leading a song ("The atmosphere is changing now, the Spirit of the Lord is here, the evidence is all around..."). The presence of God was tangible, and I could see youth clearly being impacted by the Holy Spirit. I got down on my knees at the back of the auditorium – tears flowed as I worshipped, with no one else there to see me. I too encountered God's presence in a tangible way. Pastor Brian Houston often says, "There's nothing like the presence of God." It's so true! In one moment, we both encountered the presence of God – one of us leading worship at the front, the other hiding at the back! God's presence can reach you wherever you are whenever you press into Him!

When you go through seasons of pain, make sure you don't run from God – run to Him.

TODAY:

1. Reflect on your own experiences where you have praised God through seasons of pain. Let it remind you of how His presence has been with you in the most painful moments of your life.

....

....

2. Can I encourage you to make a habit of playing worship music in your car and home? When your soul feels pain, worship attracts the presence of God and brings peace. Intentionally make space today for a Soul Time where you can kneel in His presence and encounter Him in a new way. Take time to praise God for His goodness and His faithfulness – no matter what you're currently going through.

PRAYER:

Dear Lord, I pray that despite my current circumstances, I would press into your presence. Open my eyes and ears to encounter you and not miss the moment. May I never forget how important it is to praise you, even in my time of greatest distress. You are the keeper of my soul, and you know what is best for me. I trust you, and I thank you in advance for all you will do. Amen.

DAY 7: WHEN YOUR SOUL BATTLES WITH COMPARISON

Love Melody xox

Again, it will be like a man going on a journey, who called his servants and entrusted his wealth to them. To one he gave five bags of gold, to another two bags, and to another one bag, each according to his ability.

MATTHEW 25:14-15 NIV

Do you ever feel like other people get to take a shortcut to their destination, but you still must go the long way round?

Do you ever find yourself fixated on other people's progress rather than your own?

The Parable of the Talents in Matthew 25 communicates the importance of being faithful with what God has given you. The unfaithful servant returns the exact number of talents given by the master, while the other two double their investments upon the master's return. The two who invested their talents were blessed abundantly for their faithfulness, and they were trusted with more. Generally, when we read this parable, we focus on the lesson of hard work and faithfulness. However, I want to offer another perspective – comparison.

Think about the middle servant who received two talents. He put just as much time and effort into doubling the talents as the first servant did, yet he only finished with four talents instead of ten like the other servant. The scripture says that each were given according to their abilities. I wonder how that servant felt and whether he compared himself to the other servant. Did he feel as if his abilities were "second best"? I wonder what would have happened if the second servant never knew what the first servant received. All he would have known was that the master trusted him, and then would have proceeded to generously double his talents, which is exactly what the master did for him personally.

This thought began to convict me of all the times I have selfishly fixated on counting other people's blessings from God rather than counting my own. Subconsciously, comparison causes our souls to become entangled with unhealthy patterns of jealousy, envy and a loss of joy and energy required for what we are called to do.

There's no doubt: comparison is a real soul issue in our generation. Someone is always better, prettier, smarter or richer. Even in the writing for this book, I found myself fixating on comparing myself to others who would be far more qualified to write this than I. However, it is only through battling comparison that you see how toxic it can be to your soul.

Theodore Roosevelt once said, "Comparison is the thief of joy." Comparison will cause you to lose perspective on the wonderful opportunities you have ahead of you. When you stop fixating on the progress of those around you and focus on God's plan for your own life, your soul will thrive. You have already received your own blessings and spiritual gifts from God. No ability is the "best" or "second best," so stop competing for first place. Remember, you are gifted by a generous God.

Your gift may get you to the door of opportunity, but your soul is what leads you to walk through it.

Your soul won't stand the test of time if it isn't stronger than your gift or your blessing.

TODAY:

1. Take a few moments to identify the areas in which you tend to compare yourself to others.

....

....

2. Instead of focusing on the amount of blessing that you "don't have" and comparing it to someone else's, focus on thanking God for the opportunities and blessings that you do have. Make a list of ten talents or abilities God has given you. (Go on! You do have ten!) Your soul will be happy you did.

....

....

PRAYER:

Lord, I pray you would help me each day to walk in the confidence that I am a child of God. Help me to remember your promises over my life so that I do not fall victim to comparison. I pray that your Spirit would continue to guide me on the right course for my life so that I will know without a doubt who I am and where I am meant to be. Amen.

DAY 8. WHEN YOUR SOUL NEEDS TO FEEL LOVED

It is good to proclaim your unfailing love in the morning, your faithfulness in the evening.

PSALM 92:2 NLT

What tends to be your first thought in the morning?

Your last thought at night?

We opened the *Soul Time* devotional by talking about the need for a healthy soul. A healthy soul understands how deeply, unconditionally, unreservedly and totally loved it is by God. Maybe today, you need to be reminded of how much you are loved.

Psychologists tell us that the times when we are most vulnerable to anxiety and depression or questioning our own self-worth are first thing in the morning or last thing at night. It is interesting that the psalmist, David, understood this, as he specifically encouraged the listener to proclaim His unfailing love every morning and His faithfulness every night.

It is a good thing to remind your soul first thing in the morning (before your feet touch the floor) and last thing at night (when you lay your head on the pillow), how much God loves you.

Lisa Bevere once made this incredible statement when preaching several years ago:

"God doesn't love us equally as that would mean His love could be measured. He loves His children uniquely; each person on this earth has been fashioned for the love of God."

What a thought! You are uniquely loved. He individually fashioned you in your mother's womb. Your gifts, personality and thoughts are precious to Him.

For You formed my inward parts; You covered me in my mother's womb. I will praise You, for I am fearfully and wonderfully made; Marvellous are Your works, And that my soul knows very well.... How precious also are Your thoughts to me, O God! How great is the sum of them! If I should count them, they would be more in number than the sand; When I awake, I am still with You.

PSALM 139:13-14, 17-18 NKJV, EMPHASIS ADDED

This verse tells us how valuable you are to God. He fashioned and created you. You cannot count the number of thoughts He thinks about you. He loves you this much. Your soul needs to know VERY WELL how precious you are to God.

Does your soul know very well how loved and valued you are?

If not, it's good to remind yourself. Morning and evening.

I remember when I first fell in love with Steve, who is now my husband. I experienced a feeling that no matter what my day looked like, he still loved me and thought I was awesome! It gave me a fresh confidence and subconscious reassurance that because I was loved, I could do anything! If Steve's imperfect, human love can make a positive difference in my life, how much more empowering is God's unfailing love towards you?

Your soul was created with the need to be loved by God, to be dependent on Him. When we try to do it all ourselves, in our own strength, we can be prone to feelings of self-doubt, striving or anxiety. As the psalm states today, it is important to know that God is "still with you."

If you are lying awake at night because you can't sleep, He is still with you.

If you have messed up in an area of your life, He is still with you.

Even if you feel like He is a million miles away, He is still with you.

Your soul thrives on the presence of God in your soul. Your soul needs to be with Him. "My soul yearns, even faints, for the courts of the Lord; my heart and my flesh cry out for the living God" (Psalm 84:2 NIV).

Throughout my life, I have always loved being in God's presence with other believers in church. During the COVID-19 pandemic, we had many lockdowns in England, and we couldn't physically gather as a church family. Yes, online church is great, and we thank God for it, but let's be honest – it's not the same. We realised just how much we took our churches and experiencing His presence and love for granted.

TODAY:

1. Decide to thank God for His unconditional love every morning when you wake and sip your cup of coffee or tea. Do the same thing as you pull up those covers at night.

2. Make sure you are not taking His presence or love for granted. Sit back in a chair, close your eyes and allow your heart to open to more of His presence and love for you. Meditate on His eternal and unconditional love. Make sure your soul knows "very well" how loved and valued you are by God.

PRAYER:

Lord Jesus, I pray that today, my soul will know very well that despite my failures, you love me uniquely and unconditionally, and you have amazing thoughts towards me. As I sit here, fill me with more of your love and a confident reassurance that you remain with me, enabling me to be the person you created me to be. In your name, amen.

DAY 9. WHEN YOUR SOUL HAS TRUST ISSUES

Trust in the Lord completely, and do not rely on your own opinions. With all your heart, rely on him to guide you, and he will lead you in every decision you make. Become intimate with him in whatever you do, and he will lead you wherever you go.

PROVERBS 3:5-6 TPT

Are there times when you find it a challenge to totally trust God?

When people or circumstances let you down, it can subconsciously lessen your trust in God.

Last year at church, I asked a much older lady what advice she would give to her forty-nine-year-old self. Immediately, she replied, "I'd trust God more. It all works out in the end as we keep serving him." Wise words indeed. But maybe for some of us, easier said than done in the moment!

Trusting God with the most important things in our lives, such as our family and calling, can sometimes put us to the test.

Recently, my response to a family situation caused my trust in God to waver. At the time, I didn't realise I was doing it. I was leaning on my own understanding and opinion and trying to work out a solution. I kept giving what I thought was the solution to God instead of leaving it with Him and it was stealing my inner peace.

The more you love God, the more you learn to trust Him.

A wise mentor and friend spotted it and challenged me to write a reminder note on my bathroom mirror that said, "God, I trust you with..." and fill in my concern. I felt that as a pastor and constantly helping others to trust God, I needed to be better at trusting Him for myself! Which meant to stop allowing the situation to consume my thoughts, prayers and conversations.

That week, I found myself again pouring out my heart to God in frustration and asking Him to help me trust Him more. I immediately sensed His gentle, non-judgemental response. I heard Him whisper to my heart, "My daughter, don't keep trying to trust. Just love me, just rest in my love."

We love those we trust, and we trust those we love.

What a game changer these words were! The more you love God, the more you learn to trust Him. I love the words used in The Passion Translation: *"become intimate with him in* whatever *you do and he will lead you* wherever *you go."*

What a great promise! When you are intimate with Him it affects your *whatever* and your *wherever*. Whatever you do and wherever you go. That's all encompassing. When you intimately know Him, you learn to unreservedly trust Him.

This verse also highlights His promise to *lead you* on two occasions. It promises:

He will lead you in every decision you make

He will lead you wherever you go

He will lead you! If you are struggling in the area of guidance or direction, these are great promises for you. When God repeats a principle twice in a single verse it's because He really wants you to know this truth. HE WILL LEAD YOU! In every decision and wherever you go.

We must trust God's promises **and** God's timing in our lives. It will give us a greater sense of enjoying life instead of trying to work it all out with our own understanding and opinions!

Joyce Meyer wisely says, "If your mind feels worn out all the time, you're not trusting God."[5] If you fully trusted God, what would your life look like? For me, I suspect that life would be a whole lot easier with less worry and strife, but it's always tempting to try and lend God a hand! What if we believed the following scripture? "And we know that all things work together for good to those who love God, to those who are called according to His purpose" (Romans 8:28 NIV).

Letting go of your ideals and trusting that God really does cause ALL things to work together for good is a challenge but so reassuring. The Passion Translation puts it this way: "...every detail of our lives is continually woven together to fit into God's perfect plan of bringing good into our lives, for we are His lovers who have been called to fulfil His designed purpose."

Keep focussed on loving Him with all your soul, and the rest will fall into place.

You really can trust Him with your loved ones because He loves them even more than you do. We don't have to struggle and strive. We can rest, knowing that He is in control!

TODAY:

1. Write down the things that are most important to you right now. Be prepared to let go and entrust them to God.

....

....

2. When you are tempted to get anxious, remind yourself of Romans 8:28. Say it out loud. Write it out in full, and place it beside your list of important things. Choose to focus on the truth of the scripture when each of these situations come to mind.

....

....

PRAYER:

Lord Jesus, help me to trust you with all my heart and soul, not just a small part of me. I thank you that with your help I can take the pressure off myself to try and work it all out. I can rest in your unfailing love. You will lead me, wherever I go and whatever I do. I give you those things, which are precious. I know you are working it all together for good. Amen.

DAY 10.
WHEN YOUR SOUL NEEDS TO STIR UP CREATIVITY

Love Melody xox

He [the Lord] has filled them with skill to do all kinds of work as engravers, designers, embroiderers in blue, purple and scarlet yarn and fine linen, and weavers—all of them skilled workers and designers.

EXODUS 35:35 NIV

Has the gift of creativity been allowed to become dormant in your life?

What does it mean to be creative? This is something I wrestled with during high school.

What did creation look like before it was even created? Something so versatile, yet so exquisite, that was created out of mere nothingness. Have you ever wondered about the creation of your own being? The delicate atoms that fit perfectly together to form a unique phenotype, recognising that the probability of you being created was one in 400 trillion. Yet here you are, reading what I have to say. Creation is far more than just "the process of bringing something into existence" as the dictionary defines; it is an intricate design, a divine masterpiece that has been created by a skilled creator.

I wrote this when I was in my final year of high school as part of a blog post that was never read by anyone. It stayed isolated in my laptop until I recently came across some old files. I am fascinated by the phenomenon of creation. Perhaps the most central truth about creation is that we serve such a creative God, who made us in His likeness (see Genesis 1:27).

We are both created and creative beings. Every person has the capability to create because we are made in the image of our creator. YOU were created to be creative, to reflect the creative genius of your God.

God created each of us with a soul (mind, will, emotion). Our soul allows us to connect with God. He gave us a soul so that our soul can connect with his.

Gordan Macdonald's book, *Ordering Your Private World*, explores the connection between communication, creativity and the soul. "The mind (soul) must be taught to observe and appreciate the messages God has written in creation."[6] He goes on to say that our creativity reflects the glory of God to our world.

6   Gordon Macdonald, *Ordering Your Private World,* Thomas Nelson, Nashville, p.105

Maybe you don't define yourself as a "creative" or maybe you do. Either way, I want to encourage you to stir up your creativity. We opened today's devotional with these words from Exodus: "The Lord has filled them with skill to do all kinds of work." How amazing that He has filled you with skill! This verse initially referred to the artists who were given creative talents to build the Tabernacle. In the New Testament, Ephesians 2:10 says, "For we are God's masterpiece. He has created us anew in Christ Jesus so that we can do the good things he planned for us long ago" (NLT).

You are God's work of art, God's masterpiece. Intentionally stir up the gift of creativity, which He has put within you. He has filled you with skill!

Why not create some intentional *Soul Time* to explore the creative skills and gifting God has put within you? Ask God to breathe fresh life into it. It could be song writing, art, photography, poetry, creative writing, sermon writing, pottery, photography, graphic design... there are so many ways we can be creative.

Too often, we conceal our creativity because we become too concerned with what others think. Comparison cripples our creativity. Our pride inhibits us. We need to be reminded that our gifts are God-given and are intended to be used for His glory.

One of the artists named is Bezalel (see Exodus 35:30). The name Bezalel means "in the shadow of God."

We were created to live in God's shadow; we use our gifts to place Him in the limelight.

As a worship leader, I offer my creative gifts – not so people will look at me, but so that they will worship Him. Sometimes this is an offering because you must push past what people think of you! When you use the unique gifts and abilities that He has given you, you pour them out as a creative offering to bring glory to God. When we use them for His glory, it refreshes your soul and blesses His!

TODAY:

1. Take time to appreciate God's creation. Go for a walk, watch a sunrise/sunset or take the time to look at the stars at night. Time spent in creation is great Soul Time.

2. Make a choice to do something creative during the day. Add some creativity to your mundane. It can be anything from baking a cake to writing a song or capturing a moment in creation through photography.

PRAYER:

Heavenly Father, thank you for designing me with a creative mind. I pray you would help me unleash my creativity and challenge me to try new things. You have blessed me with a great mind, and I want to steward it to the best of my ability. May I never forget how wonderfully created I am. Amen.

02. REPLENISH

PART TWO: REPLENISH

Welcome to part two in your *Soul Time* journey. This is the Soul Spa section of the holiday – the "therapy" intended to replenish, refuel and refill your soul.

"For I have satiated the weary soul, and I have replenished every sorrowful soul." After this I awoke and looked around, and my sleep was sweet to me."
JEREMIAH 31:25-26 NKJV

Our prayer is that God will "pour in" so that you can be ready to "pour out." That He will enliven your soul with a renewed passion to love God and give you the wisdom to be intentional with friendships that restore your soul. Finally, that you will be refreshed as you prepare internally for all that He has for you.

DAY 11. WHEN YOUR SOUL NEEDS A SPA

Come to Me, all you who labour and are heavy-laden, and overburdened, and I will cause you to rest. Take My yoke upon you and lean on Me, for I am gentle (meek) and humble (lowly) in heart, and you will find rest (relief and ease and refreshment and recreation and blessed quiet) for your souls.

MATTHEW 11:29 AMPC

Who would love a luxurious spa?

My hand is definitely in the air! Soothing sounds, fluffy bathrobes, relaxing steam room and beautiful aromas.

As I reflect on over thirty years in ministry, most of this was spent working "full time" and raising a family. To last over the long term, I have learned the importance of not only investing in my physical and spiritual health but also in my soul-health. On reflection, this was usually low on the agenda.

Maybe this is because I was subconsciously thinking that intentionally planning time to do things I enjoy was self-indulgent – especially when there is always so much to do in ministry and as a mum. This can be particularly true if you're the kind of person who is always looking out for everyone else.

So often, we look out for others at the expense of our own soul.

Sound familiar?

Maybe your soul needs a spa, a time of replenishing.

A replenished soul puts a spring in your step, joy in your heart and emotional fuel in your tank. You cannot keep making a difference in the lives of others if your personal fuel gauge is continually running on empty. It needs replenishing. As a family, we love a good spa for our souls! Occasionally, it's an actual spa, but mostly, it's a day that's intentionally designed to slow down, switch off, breathe and replenish the soul. It's so much more than just a day off!

Our soul spa is often a Monday (Sundays are a work day for us). In our marriage, Steve and I purposefully plan what is needed to replenish our soul and set us up for the rest of the week. When the girls weren't at school, they joined us. We began highlighting our family days on social media, which became fun for our friends to look out for. We created the *Instagram* hashtag #mawstonmonday – check it out!

When we lived in Australia, our soul spa days were often spent at the Gold Coast beaches. Here in England, we love walking in the country side, enjoying the stunning seasons, the cute seaside towns, quaint villages and hidden gem teashops. We enjoy paddle boarding on the Norfolk broads, a delicious homecooked dinner and family night with games or a movie. Some of my greatest revelations of God's Word, ideas for life and best chats with hubby happened on a Mawston Monday. Tranquillity truly breeds creativity.

Replenishing your soul is often a discipline that needs to be learned. Busyness at work is like a cancer to many a modern soul. However, the psalmist writes, "He makes me to lie down in green pastures; He leads me beside the still waters. He restores my soul" (Psalm 23:2-3 ESV). Sometimes, God must make us lie down in green pastures so that He can restore our souls. There have been times when my back has been painful, and I've had to rest physically. Sometimes, I sense that God, although He doesn't cause the pain, is making me lie down. We must stop long enough for God to restore our soul, which speeds up our physical wellbeing.

In today's scripture, Jesus tells us to learn from Him, follow His example and find refreshment for our souls. Jesus would often take time to be alone, to pull away from the crowds and the itinerary. He took time out when He was grieving, when He was tired and when He sensed He needed to be alone with His heavenly Father.

When coaching pastors and leaders, Steve and I often use the analogy of the fuel gauge on your car dashboard. This gauge tells you how much fuel you have in your tank. Fewer people pay attention to the gauge, which measures RPM'S (revs per minute).

We use the RPM'S gauge to measure how a person is doing in the four dimensions of the human personality:

- Relational
- Physical
- Mental
- Spiritual

We start each coaching session by checking in on how they are doing in each of these four areas. Usually, we ask leaders to measure how they are doing on a scale of 1-10.

It is important to pause and check your RPM'S gauge regularly. Each of these four areas are interconnected. If you are low in one of these areas, it has an impact on all the other three areas. A good soul spa invigorates all the other areas.

TODAY:

1. Have a good look at your internal dashboard. How are you doing relationally, physically, mentally and spiritually? Score yourself 1-10, and mark it in your journal. Which of your four areas needs the most attention?

....

....

2. What would a spa for your soul look like? How would you practically plan to replenish your soul? Make a list of all the things that could replenish you – a cuppa with friends, a candle-lit bubble bath, a walk in the country, a meal out.

....

....

PRAYER:

Jesus, may I learn from you about the importance of replenishing my soul. You know me better than anyone, so I want to learn from you. You want what's best for me. Please, give me the practical wisdom to replenish my soul in practical ways. In your name, amen.

DAY 12. WHEN YOUR SOUL NEEDS MORE

O God, You are my God; Early will I seek You; My soul thirsts for You; My flesh longs for You In a dry and thirsty land Where there is no water... My soul shall be satisfied as with marrow and fatness, And my mouth shall praise You with joyful lips.

PSALM 63:1, 5 NKJV

Have you ever felt both hungry and thirsty?

On the inside?

In 2008, while living in Brisbane, there was a time when I felt a strange dissatisfaction that I had never felt before. The best way to describe it is a mixture of hunger and thirst. On the inside. For several weeks, I wondered why I was feeling this way. At first, I thought it was because I was feeling homesick and missing my parents and extended family in the UK. At one stage, I decided that I needed a fun night out with girlfriends, so we went for a big night out. It was a lot of fun, but there was still something missing. I decided to splash out on some retail therapy; even a nice new pair of boots didn't take the feeling away!

During this season, I attended the 80th birthday celebration of a very dear friend, and I shared with this godly, wise lady how I was feeling. She listened to everything I was going through, and then she said something that surprised me. "Honey, you're hungry for the presence of God."

Later that evening, I was thinking about her words. I'll never forget laying back on the girls' trampoline on a balmy Brisbane evening and looking up at the stars. In that moment, I asked God to quench the thirst I was sensing in my soul with more of His love and presence. Immediately, I felt a tangible sense of God "satisfying" my soul.

I love Psalm 63 and was reminded of lyrics in a worship song I wrote many years ago:

"...when I find you, my soul is satisfied because your love is better than life, and while I breathe, I'll bless your name, living each day in the shadow of your wing." In that moment of starry solitude, I experienced first-hand the words of a promise spoken by the psalmist: "He satisfies the longing soul, and the hungry soul he fills with good things" (Psalm 107:9 ESV).

The word "satisfies" in Hebrew is *saba,* and it means "to be satisfied, fulfilled, to have one's fill, to have desire satisfied, to have in excess." I liken it to the feeling after a good Sunday roast at my mum's place with a plate filled with tender roast beef, Yorkshire puddings and loads of yummy vegetables. It's a plate full of goodness! Afterwards, I feel *saba*. Satisfied!

God sees the hunger and thirsting of your soul. He has spread a table. The roast is in the oven. The vegetables and Yorkshire puddings are ready to be served up. All you must do is respond to His invitation and be seated at His table. He satisfies us. There's more than enough!

As a result of this experience, I noticed that my desire to be intentionally in His presence grew. There was a new yearning for His Word and an expectation that He would speak to me. The fruit of this change became obvious to those close to me. My friends commented on how rested I was at the end of a busy year, when most others couldn't wait for their holidays! I noticed a new sense of ease, confidence and a contentment in my work and life.

Just as hunger or thirst drives the human body to seek out food or water, our spiritual hunger leads us to seek more of God. Nutritionists tell us we can feel hungry, but we are dehydrated and don't realise it. The psalmist, David, describes a thirsting of his soul, a longing or craving for God that brought great satisfaction and "fatness" to his soul. God will satisfy, but we must first thirst or hunger. Just as eating whets our appetite, a taste of His presence increases our desire for more. Don't feed your body and starve your soul.

Right now, we are watching people, who have not physically been in church for months, come back after a lockdown. As they step into God's presence, they worship so passionately. Tears often flow. Why? Because our soul yearns for the courts of the Lord (see Psalm 84:2). The verb "to yearn" can also mean "to ache, hunger, crave, thirst or pine." Whether we realise it or not, our soul craves, hungers and aches for the presence of God – the place where your soul is satisfied. If you haven't currently experienced this craving for God's presence or His House, perhaps you are looking, like I did, for replenishment in other futile places. In today's Soul Time, ask Him to stir up a thirst for His presence and His House.

Smith Wigglesworth once said, "The secret of spiritual success is a hunger that persists. It is an awful condition to be satisfied with one's spiritual attainments. God was and is looking for hungry, thirsty people."

TODAY:

1. I encourage you to take time to step outside, look up at the sky and ask for a greater, tangible sense of God's presence to literally fill your life, stirring up hunger and thirst for more of Him.

2. Declare verses 1 and 5 of Psalm 63 over your life. Repeat them throughout the day.

PRAYER:

Dear Lord Jesus, may my spiritual appetite for you increase in my life. May I have a hunger and a thirst for you that persists. Help me to know the difference between when my soul needs to enjoy natural things, and when my soul needs to seek you for spiritual satisfaction. Just as I enjoy great food on holiday, please fill my soul with spiritual food that will satisfy and impact every other area of my life. In your name, Jesus. Amen.

DAY 13. WHEN YOUR SOUL NEEDS A GOD-ENCOUNTER

Love Melody xox

"...that they should seek God, and perhaps feel their way toward him and find him. Yet he is actually not far from each one of us..."

ACTS 17:27 ESV

How is your soul today?

There's nothing that replenishes your soul like the presence of God. Like a God-encounter. A moment when you sense Him so close, and you are forever changed as a result. Do you remember your first encounter with God? Can you recall a life-defining moment where you felt the presence of God tangibly?

For me, I was standing in a big top tent with about one thousand other young people. It was thirty-six degrees and about ten o clock at night – the final night of a youth summer camp. I distinctly remember the presence of God in worship that night, and it was so tangible that I felt if I lifted my hands, I could physically feel the touch of God. The band was playing at full blast, yet you could still hear hundreds of voices shouting out to God. It truly was one of those pure God-encounter moments.

For several minutes, I just stopped and listened to those voices and let the noise consume me. I opened my eyes and looked around the room to see a multitude of young people with their hands raised, tears streaming down their faces and their hearts tuned into what God was saying. Everywhere I looked, every person was completely lost in worship. I continued to look across the tent, utterly amazed by the sight of young people so desperate to worship King Jesus, even during the distractions of heat and tiredness. It was breath taking.

The image of a young person who was wondering the streets completely alone popped into my mind. Another who was alone in the silence of her own house battling with insecurity and self-harm. Another resisting the pain of abuse that has swallowed him in shame. More and more of these images pierced my heart. I couldn't not be moved by the fact that I was experiencing this radical God-encounter while there were so many others who are lost and deprived of such an encounter.

As a young girl, I vowed that I never wanted to take tangible, God-encountering moments like these for granted. I decided that the presence of the Lord wasn't just an encounter that I'd only experience at a summer camp, but it was an experience that needed to be shared with every person. These divine God-encounters aren't only experienced in a big tent, but they can be found in any location if our hearts are willing.

The presence of God can be encountered in the big moments but also in the small. Through the recent season of lockdown due to a global pandemic, I have learned to also seek God in the small. In fact, I have found that creating those moments alone at home are essential to keeping my soul replenished. I pray you would never take for granted the opportunity to seek God in the mundane. There is no limit to His power and presence available in your life – just waiting for you to access. When you seek Him, you will find Him (see Jeremiah 29:13).

Do we pursue Him with a deep longing – as our vital necessity?

There are so many things competing for our hearts and our time, particularly as young adults. Can I encourage you to search for His presence as a vital necessity?

Even in the moments where His presence seems distant, we can hold on to the second half of the verse in Acts 17:27. He is not far from each one of us! We can live with a faith-filled conviction that He is always there for us, whether we feel Him or not. The memories of God-encounters and the knowledge of His nearness empower us to live with confidence, a heart for others and a regularly replenished soul.

TODAY:

1. Take 5 minutes extra in your daily devotion time to seek His presence. Pray He would speak to you as you focus your thoughts on Him.

....

....

2. Remember some of your God-encounter moments or when someone has spoken something significant into your life. By faith, thank Him that He is always close to you, never far from you, irrespective of whether you feel Him or not.

PRAYER:

Dear Lord, I ask that you would reveal yourself to me. Each day, I want to know more of you. Fill me with your revelation knowledge, and guide me with your wisdom. As I press in and seek you as a vital necessity, I know I will find you. Fill me

again with your presence. I wait on you. Amen.

DAY 14. WHEN YOUR SOUL NEEDS TO ENLARGE

Rejoice with singing, you barren one! You who have never given birth, burst into a song of joy and shout... Increase is coming so enlarge your tent and add extensions to your dwelling. Hold nothing back! Make the tent ropes longer and the pegs stronger. You will increase and spread out in every direction.

ISAIAH 54:1-3 TPT

Have you ever gone through a challenge that has stretched you so much when everything in you felt like holding back or retreating to a safe place?

I love that today's verses from Isaiah speak of enlarging and stretching at a time when the Giant of the Babylonian empire was intimidating God's people. They were in a place of restriction, far from home and experiencing great discomfort and loss. In addition, barrenness was seen as a curse and brought great shame. However, it is in the middle of this seemingly futile uncertainty that God encourages them to enlarge, grow and strengthen their stakes. External challenge and pain can either shrink or enlarge us on the inside.

The analogy of a tent refers to the Bedouin tents common in the Palestine landscape. They became family heirlooms, gradually added to as the family grew and passed down from generations. When storms came, they would have to strengthen, lengthen and add to the goat or camel hair that made up the tent's structure. They wouldn't just get a new one! A large weathered tent spoke of resilience and God's faithfulness to a family over the years.

In order to withstand the storms that life inevitably brings, I've found that your tent pegs must be safely secured. In order to "make the tent ropes longer," you need to "strengthen your pegs." Strengthening involves making sure your pegs are driven deep into the ground. You spiritually strengthen your tent pegs when you press into God – you go deeper. You literally need to "dig deep."

In 1998, Steve and I were thrilled to discover that I was pregnant with our first baby. It was such an exciting time! When we attended our 12-week scan, we couldn't wait to see our baby for the first time on the monitor. The nurse applied the gel to my tummy and started searching for baby. It seemed to take longer than we expected. The nurse called in a doctor. Now we were getting concerned. I'll never forget the doctor turning to us and with sadness in her eyes, informing us that she couldn't find our baby's heartbeat. I had miscarried.

This was the first time in my life I had experienced such intense pain and loss. I literally felt like life had been squeezed out of me. I couldn't understand how or why it happened to us. I know that this experience of loss or something similar may well have also happened to you. You'll understand the gut-wrenching pain of hopes and dreams dashed.

That evening, I read today's verses. I felt strongly that God was encouraging me to sing. Sing?! I know! It sounded crazy as I was sobbing into my pillow.

These defining moments enable you to grow through what you go through.

I certainly didn't feel like singing at a time like this. I wanted to hide away, to hold back and retreat in a safe place and grieve. I started to gently sing *Shout to the Lord* by Darlene Zschech. The lyrics describe the Lord as our comfort, refuge and strength. As I listened, I started to feel immense comfort. Even though I felt incredibly vulnerable and broken, He was my comfort and strong tower.

I was rostered to lead worship at church that weekend, and although part of me wanted to shrink back, another part of me felt like I had to dig deep and sing through my tears. Therefore, I made an intentional decision that with all the breath I had (it didn't feel like I had much!), I would worship through the tears.

When I stood up and sang these words with hundreds of others, I was amazed at how much comfort, release and strength that defining moment brought to my soul. I decided I would never again sing a worship song without meaning it from the depth of my being. I chose to dig deep.

When you choose to either physically or internally sing through the pain and the tears, you strengthen your pegs. When you choose to allow God to be your comfort, you lengthen your ropes. Your heart and soul expand again. I remember sensing the healing love of Jesus expand my heart with so much love and empathy for others experiencing loss. Don't wait until the tough time is over. Praise through the pain, and trust his steadfast love. Further down in this chapter, Isaiah reminds us of God's consistent love, "...My heart of steadfast faithful love will never leave you, and my covenant of peace with you will never be shaken" (v.10).

I genuinely believe that it's in the most private and painful places of your soul that you experience the Father's love most powerfully, and your heart grows the most if you allow it to. These defining moments enable you to grow through what you go through. The Word of God teaches us that the Lord will enlarge our hearts as we keep on obeying Him (see Psalm 119:32).

If you are going through a season of challenge, hurt or loss right now, allow God to both heal AND enlarge you on the inside to prepare you for the incredible future He has in store for you. Going through this season made me more effective as a pastor; I've literally helped countless couples through similar situations of loss.

Ask yourself: Is my heart big enough to take me where God wants me to go?

When you encounter God through the pain, He enlarges your heart so that you and your family will look back and see a story of strength, resilience and God's amazing faithfulness like those tents. Steve and I went on to have two beautiful healthy girls. Allow His love and comfort to enlarge your heart and strengthen your soul as He prepares you to be ready and more effective for all He has in your future.

TODAY:

1. Remember that God sees and understands the pain you have gone through or are in. Think of the areas in your life that need to grow despite pain or disappointment. Commit to "grow through" what you "go through."

....

....

2. Play some worship music now and sing out loud – go on! Whether it sounds good or not! Praise is releasing. Instead of overthinking, try thanking. Open your heart for God to bring healing and expand your internal capacity. Don't hold back! Don't retreat. Keep digging deep. God's got you.

PRAYER:

Lord, I ask that you would draw near to me in my pain. I thank you that you alone are my true source of lasting comfort and strength. I open my heart to your steadfast love and everlasting covenant of peace. With your help, I commit to growing through whatever I go through and enlarge my heart for you and others in the process. I thank you that nothing compares to the promise I have in you, for me and my family. Amen.

DAY 15. WHEN YOUR SOUL NEEDS TO HEAR FROM GOD

Love Melody xox

Set your gaze on the path before you. With fixed purpose, looking straight ahead, ignore life's distractions. Watch where you're going! Stick to the path of truth, and the road will be safe and smooth before you. Don't allow yourself to be sidetracked for even a moment or take the detour that leads to darkness.

PROVERBS 4:25-27 TPT

Have you ever walked through a season where it feels like God is distant?

Maybe you need an answer to prayer and some direction in your life, and you're getting nothing.

In our Christian world, we often hear people refer to "dry seasons." Seasons where God doesn't seem to speak or more likely, times when we don't hear. The truth is that God is always speaking, revealing and moving – our souls just aren't always ready to hear. This may be because we are distracted or too caught up in simply going through the motions. These seasons can cause us to get distracted from the path God has for us.

I have found myself on several occasions feeling "distant" from God.

Looking back, I have discovered that He only feels distant because of the comparison to my intimate God-encounter moments when I've felt Him so close. The truth is that we can never be "distant" from God; the moment Jesus died on the cross, He removed all our sin – the only thing that could ever separate us from God.

Though at times God may seem silent, He is never absent.

I remember, during the global COVID-19 pandemic, when I was missing church and miles away from my family in the UK, I FaceTimed my mum. She encouraged me (as she often does) by saying God is as close as I want Him to be and to reach out to Him as he is still there waiting. She inspired me to create my own worship experience – my own altar at home – and intentionally surrender to and encounter God. That night, I played worship, knelt in my bedroom and asked for God's presence to fill me again. He totally did! The Bible promises that if we draw near to God, He will draw near to us (see James 4:8). After that, I felt I started "hearing" from God again in my daily devotions and felt more certain of my path ahead.

A life with God is a life of pursuing Him relentlessly each day of our lives – even on the days we may not hear His voice in our daily *Soul Time* or during worship on a Sunday. He is still with us, and He does not stop moving. Many people ask me what to do in the dry seasons when they aren't hearing from God. It's simple: keep purposefully pursuing Him, and remove potential distractions.

Sometimes we must trust that He is with us, even when we don't feel it. Faith always triumphs over feelings.

As we focus on the path set before us and keep close to God, He will reveal what we need to do as we just keep following His footsteps. I love Pastor Bobbie Houston's book, *Stay the Path*. She encourages us to stay committed to the journey, knowing that God has already gone before you. He's already in your next month or next year, leading you forward. By staying attuned to Him, you will minimise the "dry seasons" of your life and be able to receive and hear from Him whenever that time comes. Don't forget, though at times God may seem silent, He is never absent. Remind your soul of this today, and allow His presence to replenish.

TODAY:

1. What Bible verses do you turn to when God feels distant?

....

....

2. Talk to a close friend, spouse or mentor about your daily Bible reading plan and prayer times to keep each other accountable and encouraged. Take time to physically kneel the next time you pray, and surrender your life to Him afresh.

PRAYER:

Dear Lord, I pray that you would help me not to get distracted from hearing your voice. I thank you that even in the seemingly dry seasons, you never leave me. I want to stay close. I open my heart and soul to hear whatever you have to say. Speak Lord, your servant is listening. I commit to staying the path with you as your recharge my soul along the way. Amen.

DAY 16. WHEN YOUR SOUL NEEDS TO LOVE

You shall LOVE the Lord your God with ALL your heart, with ALL your soul, and with ALL your strength. And these words I command you today shall be in your heart.

DEUTERONOMY 6:5-6 NKJV (EMPHASIS ADDED)

Have you ever asked yourself how you can love God more?

This was a question a young adult asked me several years ago. She had heard countless sermons calling her to love God more. She sometimes compared herself to others, who seemed to have a closer relationship with God. As a result, she felt under pressure to love Him more. She knew that she had drifted a little in her relationship with God and was sensing a need to replenish her love for God. But how do you do this practically?

Before I share with you the answer I gave to her question, allow me to share a scripture that has really helped me and some of my own experiences growing up: "Now hope does not disappoint, because the love of God has been poured out in our hearts by the Holy Spirit who was given to us" (Romans 5:5 NKJV).

I've learned that genuinely loving God doesn't happen through our own human efforts. We need supernatural help from the Holy Spirit. He is often described in the Bible as our "helper."

I remember being filled with the Holy Spirit as a young girl at a conference in our church. Immediately, I felt a surge of love towards my friends and those who didn't know Jesus. After this experience, my cousin and I went around telling everyone who would listen how much the Holy Spirit had changed us! I didn't have to work at this – it simply happened. It's as if God's love was poured into me and then flowed out of me.

A few years later, I left the safety and security of a loving Christian family and headed to university. I shared a house with three girls who were not Christians. They became great friends, but they made very different lifestyle choices to me. I remember one night when I declined their invitation to go clubbing and drinking with them. They meant well, but it just wasn't my scene. I found myself sitting on my bed, feeling excluded and lonely. I cried out to God, wondering if I had what it took to love God and live a life that pleased Him. As I prayed, I literally felt God fill my room with His presence. I sensed His love in a tangible way.

This experience made a huge impact on me. I felt as if He refilled and replenished my love for Jesus. I still get goosebumps when I think about it. This pouring out of God's love guided me through the three years away from home. The Holy Spirit really is a great helper! He helped me have the confidence to make wise choices and empowered me to share my faith.

Decades later, when I was asked by the young adult about how to love God more, I pointed her to this experience of my fresh encounter of the love of God. His love acts as a compass; it centres and guides us. When His replenishing love is poured into our heart by the Holy Spirit, we love Him in return, and it stops us from drifting from Him.

God's *agape* love is pure, selfless, sacrificial and unconditional. There-fore, if we want to love God more, we shouldn't try to do it ourselves or try and earn His love. We can simply ask him! The Holy Spirit then pours out the love of God into our hearts so that we can give it out to others.

The Bible teaches in 1 John 4:18 that perfect love casts out *all* fear. The fear of letting God down. The fear of not measuring up or loving Him enough.

Perfect love is not our love for Him – it's His love for us.

This takes the pressure off us! We may not always feel God's love in a tangible way like I did in my bedroom as a young girl. However, we can daily believe by faith that the Holy Spirit pours God's love into us so that it can flow through us to others. Sometimes you don't feel it, but you can still believe it. When we place our faith in Him and the fact that He loves us so much, it helps us to love others unconditionally and sacrificially.

When the religious rule keepers were putting pressure on Jesus and trying to trap Him and complicate the issue, Jesus quoted today's scripture from Deuteronomy 6:5-6. I love it in The Passion Translation: "Love the Lord your God with every passion of your heart, with all the energy of your being, and with every thought that is within you" (Matthew 22:37).

Keep it simple. Keep Jesus at the centre of your soul's passions. The more you love God, the more you will love others. Thankfully, we can do this with the help of the Holy Spirit. "Relax, everything's going to be all right; rest, everything's coming together; OPEN YOUR HEARTS, LOVE IS ON THE WAY!" (Jude 1:2 MSG, emphasis added).

TODAY:

1. How can you avoid the trap of feeling pressured to earn God's love or question His love when you can't feel it?

....

....

2. Write out Jude 1:2 in the Message version and declare it. Take a few moments to relax and rest. Open your heart, and ask the Holy Spirit to pour out more of the love of God into your soul.

....

....

PRAYER:

Lord Jesus, my desire is to love you more. Please, through your Holy Spirit, fill my soul, my energy, passions and thoughts with more of your love so that I can love you more. As I love you, help me to love those around me – especially those who I am struggling to love in my own strength. I thank you that I can relax in that love and know that everything is going to be alright – that it is all coming together. Thank you for loving me. Amen.

DAY 17. WHEN YOUR SOUL NEEDS TO DREAM

Love Melody xox

Daniel had a dream, and visions passed through his mind as he was lying in bed. He wrote down the substance of his dream.

DANIEL 7:1 NIV

What is your biggest dream?

What about those crazy ideas that pop into your mind? Or like Daniel, maybe you have dreams while you sleep?

Or maybe you no longer dream. Your soul has forgotten how to. Life and its disappointments can knock the dreams out of us, before we even start to achieve them.

Dreams can help to fuel your soul. They keep us passionate and intentional.

In order to recharge your soul for this next season, let me ask you a question: What makes you jump-off-your-seat passionate and excited for the future?

I have always been a dreamer and always recorded my dreams. Perhaps there's a longing deep within all of us for a God-given dream to become reality. I find that writing my dreams down is the first step in trusting God to turn them into a potential reality. As a young child, it was the adventures of Sharkboy and Lavagirl that fuelled my obsession with a "dream journal." As I got older, it was probably my mum's influence. In Habakkuk 2:2, the prophet encourages us to write down the vision and make it plain so that those who read it can run and take action.

Two of the Bible's dreamers, Joseph and Daniel, exemplify the importance of God-given dreams. They were both just teenagers when God gave them dreams. Their dreams seemed impossible, but through these two dreamers, God worked out His purposes in the nation.

What is the God-dream for your life? The dream that will bring honour and glory to Him? The dream He has planted in your heart?

I remember attending Colour Conference with my mum in Sydney when I was 14 years old. I was so inspired by all the messages and seeing Hillsong Young and Free lead worship. God spoke to me and birthed a deep desire and calling to lead others in worship. I wrote this in my Dream Journal. At the time, it seemed like a crazy kind of dream. I wrote that one day I would love to sing and travel with Young and Free. It seemed like an impossible dream back then, but in 2019, that dream became a reality – I was asked to travel and sing with Young and Free on their USA tour. It was an honour, an incredible life-dream-come-true-experience for which I will always be grateful.

I believe writing it down was a start. I also believe that serving week in and week out in church and being faithful with what God had put in my hand helped to make what was in my heart a reality.

Recently, I received a journal that encouraged me to write my "top 100 dream bucket list." I found it challenging at first. However, as I began to write down my dreams, more and more just kept coming. I know that not all our dreams are God dreams. I prayed over them and asked that God's will be done in and through me. I committed them to Him!

I believe that writing down your dreams, praying over them and taking small daily steps can guide you into your God-given future.

Ecclesiastes 5:3 says a dream comes with much activity. Writing it down is the start. Being faithful and pursuing your dream often takes much longer, just as the life of Joseph proves!

My prayer is that you would recharge your soul by dreaming some of the God dreams for your life. If there were no limitations, what would your dream be?

TODAY:

1. Write down a dream you believe God has given you. If you're feeling outrageous, create a "top 10 dream bucket list." Pray over those dreams and commit them to God.

....

....

2. Plan practical steps you can start consistently making towards achieving one of your dreams.

....

....

PRAYER:

Dear Lord, I pray that you would continue to stir up a passion in me to pursue the dreams you have for my life. Help me to discern what your plan is for my life and not just my agenda. Reveal to me the steps I can take. May I have the courage and the faith to pursue the dreams you have placed within me. May any desire that is not of you be taken away. I trust you with my whole life, and I pray you would bring your will for my life into fruition. Amen.

DAY 18.
WHEN YOUR SOUL NEEDS REFRESHING FRIENDSHIPS

Love Melody xox

Sweet friendships refresh the soul and awaken our hearts with joy, for good friends are like the anointing oil that yields the fragrant incense of God's presence.

PROVERBS 27:9 TPT

Do you have friends that always leave you feeling better about yourself after you have been with them?

Have you ever felt drained or exhausted after spending time with people who are meant to be your friends?

My younger sister recently came to me after some issues with her teenage friends. I smiled as I remembered being in similar situations when I was in school. I also had a similar conversation with a 26-year-old friend of mine who is experiencing similar dramas in her friendships. I was disappointed to discover that friendship issues and dramas exist in your twenties as well as the teens! We are all human and imperfect. Therefore, the Bible encourages us to be wise and intentional when it comes to the gift of friendship.

Proverbs 27:9 describes sweet friendships that can replenish, refresh and restore your soul. These friendships awaken your heart with joy! What are the most important facets of true friendship, and how can we choose meaningful relationships that help to replenish our soul? For our *Soul Time* today, I have compiled what I think are the three most important facets of true friendship and how each of us can find rich and meaningful relationships that help to replenish our soul.

Firstly, great friends carry the sweet smell of unity! Great friends carry a pleasant fragrance. The Mawston family are very competitive, especially when we play Killer Uno. My dad will wind us up when he wins by referring to the "sweet smell of success." Success may or may not have a sweet smell, but good friendships do.

How truly wonderful and delightful it is to see brothers and sisters living together in sweet unity! It's as precious as the sacred scented oil flowing from the head of the high priest Aaron.

PSALM 133:1-2 TPT

Good friends bring unity and a great smell. When some friends enter the room, they leave a pleasant odour. You feel better for being with them. They leave a deposit in the atmosphere of your soul. They build you up and encourage you. These are great friends to have in your life. Other friends bring a very different smell to the room. Gossip, negativity and put-downs leave an ugly scent that no one wants to be around.

Secondly, great friends speak sweet words of forgiveness. Choose friends who know how to speak sweet words. The dictionary's definition of "sweet" includes "pleasant, delightful, easy to like, attractive." Sweet words make your heart glad; they refresh your soul. These are the friends we need to have and the friend we need to be. Some of the sweetest words that friends can ever say are "I'm sorry" and "I forgive you." Forgiveness is essential for refreshing friendships. Letting things drag on will drain your soul. We must be willing to forgive those who have hurt us. With love comes hurt. We are to forgive other because the Lord has forgiven us (see Colossians 3:13).

Thirdly, great friends draw you into God's presence. Do your friends attract and draw you into the presence of God and the things of God? Or do you find they draw you further away? Look for the friends that encourage you when you're weary and remind you of your God dreams and calling.

Generous people refresh others and in return, they are also refreshed (see Proverbs 11:25). Generosity isn't just about giving money; you can be generous in friendships. When you are generous in friendships, you are thinking about the other person more than yourself.

When you are a friend that restores and refreshes others, you'll find your friendships will restore and replenish you.

PART I – REST

Be the first person in your friendship circle to be this replenishing friend. Don't let your friendship drama or social politics distract you from pursuing real, genuine and authentic friendship. When you spread Christ's love throughout your friend-ships or your comments on social media, you will leave behind a sweet aroma.

Choose sweet friends that refresh your soul, and be that kind of friend to those around you.

TODAY:

1. Who are your sweet friends that draw you closer to God and replenish your soul? Send them a message to highlight the qualities you appreciate about them.

....

....

2. How can you be more intentional about attracting people closer to God through friendship? Which of your friends don't know Jesus? What could you do to leave a sweet-smelling deposit in their life today?

....

....

PRAYER:

Lord, I pray that your Spirit would guide me and give me dis-cernment to choose friends who replenish my soul. I ask that you would help me to model what it means to be an intentional refreshing, uncomplicated and encouraging friend to others. I pray that I would model your love and kindness throughout every aspect of my friendships today. Amen.

DAY 19. WHEN YOUR SOUL NEEDS TO FLOURISH

Love Melody xox

Those who are planted in the house of the LORD Shall flourish in the courts of our God. They shall still bear fruit in old age; They shall be fresh and flourishing,

PSALM 92:13-14 NKJV

What does it mean to "flourish"?

The dictionary's definition of this word includes "to grow or develop in a healthy or vigorous way, especially as the result of a particularly congenial environment." I believe that your life is supposed to be fruitful and healthy. What does it mean for our souls to flourish? And what is our congenial environment?

All my life, I have been planted in the church. I am passionate and excited about being in church. I've learned that the church isn't just a building or its geographical location, but the church is wherever the people are. We have moved from city to city and country to country as I was growing up, and I still always found my community within the church.

My parents have always taught me the importance of being planted in the House of God; they were taught by their parents, and my grandparents were taught by their parents. Many generations of our family knew the value and importance of being planted in the House of God. We never missed a single Sunday in the building. Even when we were on holidays, we wouldn't miss it. My sister and I would force our parents to come back from holidays early so we could be there in time for Friday night youth. Through the eyes of a child, church was a party every single weekend with God and all your best friends. I have been blessed by serving at church all these years, and I can say without a doubt that I have flourished and seen those around me flourish as well.

My dad often says that if you want something to flourish, make sure you plant it in the House of the Lord. If you want your kids to flourish, plant them in the House of the Lord. if you want your finances to flourish, plant them in the House of the Lord. If you want your gifts to flourish, plant them in the House of the Lord.

My mum reminded me recently about a scripture she received for me and my sister, Mercy, many years ago. She was in the process of making a big decision. I was eight years old at the time. She said she had been praying and that God had spoken to her, reassuring her that her children will live in security and thrive in His presence (see Psalm 102:28). I can honestly say that being raised in and around God's house, with godly people, has caused my life to thrive as I've grown in confidence and security.

I wonder what your experience of church is? You may not have had the same experience that I have had in being brought up in a Christian family and a great church. Recently, I have been motivated to encourage others to set the example and be the church of which they want to be a part. Imagining the church as we did as kids, where we had these incredible God encounters and that was all that mattered. Humans are flawed and no one can be perfect, but it is our job to set the example that the Bible instructs us to do. And that is to stay planted in the House of the Lord.

From now on, make it your priority to be part of a church that keeps Jesus in the centre and encourages you to use your gifts to make a difference. Be the encouraging, life-giving atmosphere. It will keep your soul replenished, secure and confident.

If our main goal as Christians is to serve the Lord and to make disciples, then what better place to do this than in the House of God? His House really is the hope for hurting humanity. My prayer for you is that your heart and soul will find a place of planting and belonging. A place where you can be excited to go to be replenished and to serve the Lord.

Your soul will keep flourishing when you keep choosing to stay planted in God's House.

TODAY:

1. Show your appreciation to your church leaders by sending a message or an email to your pastor or oversight. Tell them one thing from their church ministry that you are thankful because it has impacted you.

....

....

2. Decide today to increase your excitement for going to church. Think about the gifts that you have and how you could put them to use in God's House.

....

....

PRAYER:

Lord, thank you for blessing me with a church to call home. I pray that even in the tough times you would help me to stay planted so that my soul can flourish. Help me to remember just how blessed I am to be able to publicly serve and worship you in my church, in a world where many churches are persecuted. Help my soul to never take for granted the opportunity I have. Amen.

DAY 20. WHEN YOUR SOUL NEEDS A SHOT OF PASSION

Be enthusiastic to serve the Lord, keeping your passion toward him boiling hot! Radiate with the glow of the Holy Spirit and let him fill you with excitement as you serve him.

ROMANS 12:11 TPT

How would you rate your current level of passion for life?

I love the word passion! Your soul holiday can be a great opportunity to experience a fresh infusion of passion. The dictionary definitions of the word "passion" are fascinating.

Firstly, the word "passion" can be described as "a powerful or compelling emotion, a strong love, or an extravagant fondness, enthusiasm, or desire for something or someone."People who live with passion are some of the most attractive people on the planet. They are enthusiastic and lifegiving, and their magnetism is contagious. I love being around them.

Who wouldn't want to be a person full of passion?

Sadly, life has many ways of pouring water on our passion. Negativity neutralises passion. Prevailing culture can kill passion. Discouragement drains us of our passion. Like a nail embedded in the wheel of a car tyre, our passion can slowly seep out from our soul.

This brings us back to another definition of the word "passion." Most dictionaries refer to the "passion of Christ." When you trace the history of the meaning of this word (its etymology), it comes from the Latin *passionem* meaning "suffering and enduring." It literally means "that which must be endured."

... let us run with endurance the race that is set before us, looking unto Jesus, the author and finisher of our faith, who for the joy that was set before him endured the cross, despising the shame, and has sat down at the right hand of the throne of God.

HEBREWS 12:1B-2 (NKJV)

Jesus demonstrated *passionem*. He suffered and endured the cross and its shame. We can become so familiar with the story of the cross that we forget the depth of the rejection and the physical and emotional pain He endured. At His agonising moment of saving the world, even His own Father turned His back on Him, as He could not look at sin. Jesus, fully man, endured His present pain by focussing on His future joy. Jesus had a goal in mind. It was you. He knew His death would accomplish incredible future freedom for us, His people.

How do we endure seasons of pain and stay passionate? By looking unto Jesus and learning from Jesus. When we are passionately focused on Him, then we endure, we overcome, we finish the race!

The first pandemic lockdown period of 2020 tested my ability to endure. My personal level of passion slowly depleted. Many of the things, which normally refill my tank (being with people, God's House, spas, restaurants, travel) were cancelled or unavailable. As a result, I felt my energy levels deplete. A lack of passion results in a lack of energy and zest for life. I went out for a walk to sort myself out as I often did during lockdown. I found myself thinking about my favourite verse as a child: "Delight yourself in the Lord and He will give you the desires of your heart. Commit your way to the Lord, trust also in Him, and He shall bring it to pass" (Psalm 37:4-5 NKJV).

To my amazement, the word "delight" in Hebrew means "to pamper or refresh oneself, to take pleasure in." When we delight ourselves in the Lord, it is literally like having a spa. You just feel better in your soul! Your external circumstances may not change, but the condition of your soul is refreshed and recharged.

Then I checked the word "delight" in the dictionary: "A high degree of gratification, joy, like a child squealing with delight." This reminded me of a little child feeling delight at seeing her father. The next day, I went on another walk, already feeling more passionate. I remembered these scriptures and purposefully did a little skip (don't laugh).

Sometimes in life, we have little control over what happens to us, but we can take responsibility for what happens in us, in our soul.

Be aware of the level of passion in your soul. Life motivation comes from the deep longings of the heart (and soul), and a renewed internal passion will keep you moving forwards towards the deepest longings of your soul (see Proverbs 16:26).

TODAY:

1. Take time to go for a walk and think about what it means for you to delight in God. Delight in His character, His promises, His faithfulness and His unconditional love for you. You could even try a little skip if no one is looking! It can work wonders!

2. What areas of your life need a shot of passion? Ask God to inject fresh passion for the things that may have become mundane or challenging. Your relationship with God? Your close relationships? Your work? Your giftings? Your role in church? Your business? Jot them down in your journal. Choose to intentionally focus on Jesus by meditating on Hebrews 12:1- 3.

....

....

PRAYER:

Lord Jesus, I pray that as a delight in you, look to you and learn from you, that you would increase my passion. May I be passionate about the things that you are passionate about. I thank you that as you light up my delight, you will give me the desires of my heart. You are my energy! May I inspire others with my passion for you and for life. I love you, Jesus. Amen.

03. RECHARGE

PART THREE: RECHARGE

Now that you have rested and replenished, the final purpose of your *Soul Time* is to reinvigorate and inspire you to dream again and take courageous steps to move forwards in your calling.

Help me turn my eyes away from illusions so that I pursue only that which is true; drench my soul with life as I walk in your paths. Reassure me of your promises, for I am your beloved.
PSALM 119:37 TPT

May your soul be drenched with life as you choose to walk in His paths prepared for you.

You can't be fully recharged to step into your next season without the confidence to apply what God has shown you. Melody and I have purposefully included two days about the topic of confidence to conclude this section because we know how essential this is for us girls! Our prayer is that you will be reignited and recharged to pursue the promises of God for your life and make sure you enjoy the journey!

DAY 21. WHEN YOUR SOUL NEEDS ASSURANCE OF YOUR CALLING

...who has saved us and called us with a holy calling, not according to our works, but according to His own purpose and grace which was given to us in Christ Jesus before time began,

2 TIMOTHY 1:9 NKJV

Do you have a confident conviction that you are called by God?

Are you allowing His call to shape and direct your life?

Now that you are resting and replenishing on your soul holiday, maybe today's *Soul Time* is the perfect moment to remember and refresh the sense of calling on your life. Regularly remembering and redefining the call of God on your life keeps you anchored and moving forwards with confidence.

The first time I realised God was giving me a sense of calling was as a 12-year-old girl attending a Christian concert in St. Andrews Hall, Norwich with my friends from school. I remember seeing most of my unchurched friends respond to the invitation at the end to receive Jesus and make Him Lord of their lives. I felt a deep sense of compassion for them, and my heart was moved with the realisation of how this moment could potentially impact their lives for eternity. Through tears that night, I sensed a strong sense of calling to devote my life to helping others become followers of Jesus through preaching, worship and pastoring. This strong sense of calling set the direction of my life.

At a particularly difficult crossroads in my life, one Sunday afternoon, I was walking around the park near our home in Brisbane. I literally felt the Holy Spirit come and walk alongside me. He gave me flashbacks of incidents, which occurred throughout my whole life – like a highlights reel. He literally showed me how His hand had been on me life throughout my childhood and teenage years and how He had set me apart to communicate His Word. Throughout this journey, I could see how I had constantly doubted my own ability. As the Holy Spirit took me on this journey, I physically felt my lips become burning hot as I recalled the passage from Isaiah chapter 6, which describes how Isaiah is called to speak and he doesn't feel good enough. God takes a burning coal from the altar and touches his lips (see Isaiah 6:8).

I knew this was a significant moment and life-defining moment of calling. I was literally weeping as I walked home. I knelt in my living room and surrendered my role, my family and my future to God. It was a holy moment I'll never forget. From that moment on, I knew that part of my life calling and anointing is preaching His Word and helping others do the same.

Maybe you have not had a dramatic encounter calling like this moment that I have described. Recognising God's call is often a process of discovery and can take years for some people. Oz Guinness in his book, *The Call,* was a great help to me in defining God's calling. Guinness says our primary call is to know God, and our secondary or vocational call is how we outwork that in making a difference in others' lives. He emphasises "secondary callings matter only because primary calling matters most."[7] However, primary calling must always lead to secondary calling. Secondary calling is discovering our life's purpose.

To live knowing you are called by God is the most empowering, meaningful, capacity-enlarging, joy-giving, contagious, purpose-driven feeling on earth!

Can I encourage you that calling is not just limited to a church setting? It can include any sphere of influence where you can use your gifts for His glory. You may not feel good enough like I did, and life may bring some

---

7   Os Guinness, The Call. Finding and Fulfilling the Central Purpose of Your Life. Thomas Nelson, Nashville. p.31

unexpected turns. But reminding yourself of God's calling on your life will keep your soul anchored.

Paul, in his letter to young Timothy, reminds him to not only live "saved" but also to live life "called." According to 2 Timothy 1:9, you are saved AND called. Pastor Brian Houston constantly encourages us to not just live "saved" but to also live life as if we are "called." It is a holy calling – a calling that comes from God Himself.

Timothy had been pastoring the church in Ephesus at a time of intense persecution under the ruthless Emperor Nero. Paul himself is on the brink of losing his own life. Yet he challenges Timothy to stir up the gift within him and not forget his calling, even though life all around him is full of challenge and opposition (see 2 Timothy 1:6). I'm sure Timothy felt inadequate and too young at times.

Sometimes, opposition or intimidation causes us to step back, to choose comfort over calling. We need to stir up the gifts, which God has so graciously given us. His calling on our lives is always according to His purpose, and His grace will always enable.

Ephesians 2:10 says, "For we are His workmanship, created in Christ Jesus for good works, which God prepared beforehand that we should walk in them" (NKJV). This verse teaches several truths about your call-ing. You are His workmanship. I love that thought. Like a valuable piece of furniture, you have been handcrafted by God Himself. Not only does this make you incredibly valuable, but the Greek word for workmanship is *poeima* from which we get the word "poem." A poem is an original work of art. You are a one-off. Unique! There is nobody on planet earth quite like you.

You are the only person with your unique combination of skills, person-ality and gifting who can impact the people in your world in the way that you can. When you live "called" you are acknowledging that these gifts come from God and you desire to use them for Him. When you function in this unique calling and start helping others, you will find your greatest reward and fulfilment in life.

To step into that calling and have the privilege of seeing all or part of it fulfilled is what dreams and destinies are made of. It's what you were created for! Your soul will feel such enjoyment and fulfilment; you will feel like you're on holiday.

Your calling gives you an ability to say with conviction, "No matter what, I'll never give up. Whatever comes my way, I'll stand. If I don't succeed, I'll try again. If I'm criticised, I'll rise above it."

You are called by God. You are born for greatness. Circumstances may change, you may change, but the call of God on your life does not change. When you feel frustrated, remind your soul that you are called by God and that every detail of His purpose for your life will reign supreme (see Ephesians 1:10 TPT).

Keep reminding your soul, you are called by God!

TODAY:

1. Remind yourself of a time when your heart was stirred to follow God's call. Where were you? What did God say to you?

....

....

2. Complete the following in one sentence: God has called me to ...

....

....

PRAYER:

Lord, I thank you that I am not only saved but called. The call of God is on my life. I thank you for those moments when I felt the sense of your call on my life. I surrender my heart and soul, my dreams and plans to you again. I ask that you will continue to remind me of my calling with fresh clarity as I step forward. In Jesus' name, amen.

DAY 22. WHEN YOUR SOUL NEEDS TO DREAM AGAIN

Never doubt God's mighty power to work in you and accomplish all this. He will achieve infinitely more than your greatest request, your most unbelievable dream, and exceed your wildest imagination! He will outdo them all, for his miraculous power constantly energizes you.

EPHESIANS 3:20 TPT

Do you have dreams that are yet to be fulfilled? Have you been disappointed that a dream you thought would happen, just didn't work out? Have you forgotten your dream or laid it aside?

As you read yesterday (Day 21), God has saved and called you. But what does the call of God look like for you in practical terms? I am convinced God created us to dream, and they form a large part of how we outwork our calling and purpose.

God's Word clearly tells us that He can accomplish things beyond our dreams and exceed even our wildest imagination. This is probably one of the most popular and often quoted verses in the Bible, but we can often forget the second part. In the NKJV it says "according to the power that works in us." It starts when we allow His power to work in us. However, this is not always easy when life doesn't go to plan. Our plan!

In the Bible, Joseph was a dreamer, but as a young man, his dreams of destiny and calling were put on hold for seventeen years. Joseph was thrown into a pit by his jealous brothers, human trafficked into slavery, wrongly accused of rape, imprisoned and forgotten. Joseph's dream must have seemed so far away. I wonder whether you have ever felt that your dreams seem more like a pipe dream or a mirage in the desert.

When Joseph miraculously sees his brothers again, he doesn't try to get even, he doesn't have a massive pity party, he doesn't even question God. "And he remembered the dreams he'd had about them many years before. " (Genesis 42:9 NLT). Instead, the scripture says *he remembered the dreams.*If Joseph remembered his dreams, it's probably because he had forgotten them. Discouragement and disappointment can cause you to forget your dreams instead of believing in them.

Despite the opposition and disappointment that he faced throughout his life, Joseph's dreams really did come to pass. He lived it! Joseph became the second most powerful man in Egypt. His God-given authority

PART 3 – RECHARGE

enabled him to not only provide for his family but to save the known world from starvation! That's a big dream fulfilled!

Maybe as you read this you are thinking, "That's great for Joseph, but what about my dream?" Maybe like Joseph, you find it easier to forget your dream than face the regret of your unfulfilled dreams. Earlier in the devotional, we looked at the importance of having a dream, but it's also important that we need to learn to dream again. We can sometimes forget our dreams, and we need to stir them up afresh. It's easier to shrink back and accept your current reality than risk the pain of unfulfilled dreams.

I read a sobering article by an Australian palliative care nurse, Bonnie Ware, entitled *5 Regrets of the Dying*. Bonnie interviewed hundreds of people as they embraced their last moments on earth and reflected on their lives. The top regret of the dying was, "I wish I had the courage to live a life true to myself and not the life others expected of me." Most confided that they faced dying in the knowledge that the choices they made had not honoured even half of their dreams.

All of us can probably relate to this in some way. For me personally, when a dream nurtured for many years didn't happen, my disappointment was painful. But God graciously took my unfulfilled dream and redirected us into a new adventure. Although it was not the dream I expected, we moved back to our roots in Norwich to be part of the senior leadership team at the dynamic Soul Church. Steve and I also have the honour of coaching pastors and leaders and preaching in churches across the UK and beyond.

However, during a pivotal conversation with my friend and mentor, Margaret Stunt, she helped me see that because of previous disappointments, where a long-time dream had seemingly come to an end, I'd stopped dreaming. I had slowly settled into my present and helping others, when finally, I admitted I was too scared to dream again for my future in case it didn't happen. I'd stopped articulating and writing down my dreams, which I'd regularly done throughout my life and had encouraged others to do also. I had subconsciously built a wall of self-preservation around my soul. I felt challenged to seek God again, stir up the dreams He had put deep within my soul and get my journal out again!

A dream is the calling, destiny and future that God has for you. It can sometimes feel so distant that many people give up along the way. It requires a courageous journey of self-discovery and dependence on God. Don't settle – you'll become stagnant if you don't have a dream.

A dream stirs you from your comfort zone and inspires you to step into your faith zone.

If you want to soar beyond your present and embrace the power of your possible future, why not take the time to write your dream down? The prophet, Habakkuk, inspires us to do this: "Write the vision (dream), make it plain. So that the one who reads it will run. For the vision (dream) is yet for an appointed time, it will not fail. Even though it delays, wait for it, because it will certainly come; it will not delay" (see Habakkuk 2:2).

- Write it.
- Read it.
- Run with it!

TODAY:

1. Did you once have a dream that you have forgotten? Why do you think you forgot your dream? What are the dreams you've had in your heart that have been delayed or derailed?

....

....

2. Like Joseph, it's time to remember your dream. Grab your pen and journal and go to a peaceful spot. Use your Soul Time today to get ready to dream again. Visualise your dreams, write them down and share them with someone you trust. Read them regularly so that you can keep taking steps forwards. Keep praying over them and believe God to exceed your wildest imagination!

PRAYER:

Lord, I ask that you would stir up dreams in my heart and soul that may have become dormant or forgotten. I choose to let go of disappointment. I trust that you will energise me, as your Word says, to remember the dream, which you have put in my heart. Guide me as I write them down, and I thank you that you can do more than I can ask or think. I ask this in your name, amen.

DAY 23. WHEN YOUR SOUL NEEDS PURPOSE

Since we are approaching the end of all things, be intentional, purposeful, and self-controlled so that you can be given to prayer. Above all, constantly echo God's intense love for one another, for love will be a canopy over a multitude of sins.

1 PETER 4:7-8 TPT

How much of your day-to-day life is in line with your purpose?

Identifying your calling and dream is crucial. The next step is to pursue them intentionally and purposefully.

It's easy to start drifting through life – to allow your days to be determined by other people's agenda or priorities. The Oxford dictionary defines "intentionality" as "the fact of being deliberate or purposeful."

There's a big difference between good intentions and God intentions. True purpose is aligned with the call of God because He created us, gifted us and knows what's best for our lives.

While it's important to be there for others, Peter encourages us to live our lives purposefully and intentionally in order to move forwards. The decision to be intentional and purposeful is an internal one. Using your *Soul Time* is a great way to re-evaluate this.

Life is more fruitful and your soul much healthier when you live by design and not default.

Jesus clearly directed his time between preaching to the crowds, healing individuals and preparing His disciples to carry on His purpose after He ascended to heaven. His strong sense of cause enabled Him to plan and use His time well (see Mark 1:38 NKJV).

Jesus lived intentionally with a deep sense of purpose.

How can you live your life with a sense of purpose?

I have always been determined, a quiet achiever by nature. But I've learned that intentionality is much more than a personality type.

My life became much more intentional after reading John Maxwell's book, *Intentional Living*. He prioritises placing value on every person he encounters daily because this is part of his life's purpose. In order to achieve this, Maxwell emphasises the importance of a daily routine: "The secret of your success is determined by your daily agenda."[8]

What do you do every day that helps you step towards your purpose and calling? Now is a great time to redefine and articulate your purpose.

As I write this, Steve and I are about to celebrate 28 years of marriage. One of the reasons our marriage has been so strong is that we have been very intentional about building an excellent marriage. Twenty-five years ago, we were inspired by Pastor Brian Houston's vision for Hillsong Church, *The Church I See*. We decided to write a vision statement for our marriage. We called it *The Marriage We See*. A great marriage isn't fluked, it's built. Without a doubt, this is one of the best things we have ever done as a married couple.

One of the lines we included was that we wanted "to build a marriage that was an example to other young people." Over the last 25 years, we have lost count of the number of people who have come up to us and said that they would love to have a marriage like ours one day. This is because we were highly intentional with our marriage; we chose to build it by design and not default.

---

8   John Maxwell, *Intentional Living*, Center Street, New York, p. 42

TODAY:

1. If you were honest, how much of your life are you living intentionally in light of your purpose? What are the key things, which are distracting you from your purpose?

....

....

2. What is one thing you could do daily in order to be more intentional?

....

....

NOTE: For those of you who would like to pursue this in greater depth, I have included 5 questions I ask myself and journal daily in the Delve Deeper section for Day 23.

PRAYER:

Dear Jesus, help me to be more intentional with my day. Help me to know and understand the purpose you have for me. Give me the wisdom to ignore distractions and to live with a sense of direction and calling. Help me to manage my time effectively. Thank you for giving me the Holy Spirit to lead and nudge me in the right direction. May I walk in obedience to your voice, your nudges and my purpose throughout this day. In Jesus' name, amen.

DAY 24. WHEN YOUR SOUL NEEDS A GOAL

...it is my ONE aspiration]: forgetting what lies behind and STRAINING FORWARD to what lies ahead, I press on toward the GOAL to WIN the [supreme and heavenly] prize to which God in Christ Jesus is CALLING us upward. So let those [of us] who are spiritually mature and full grown have this mind and hold these convictions.

PHILIPPIANS 3:13-15 AMPC (EMPHASIS ADDED)

Have you ever felt like your life is being lived on a treadmill and not going anywhere?

It's one of the most frustrating feelings. Maybe as you have reflected on your life during *Soul Time*, you can see that you got side-tracked from your calling and your dream. You have recognised the need to live intentionally and with purpose but haven't set yourself any realistic goals to keep you on track.

Psalm 23 is probably the most well-known Psalm in the Bible and is familiar to many. It shows the connection between our soul and moving forward in life, referring to the Lord leading us in paths of righteousness (see verse 3). The Shepherd not only restores our soul – He also *leads* us. He leads us in new paths, new pastures with a new sense of purpose and passion for what lies ahead.

The Apostle Paul was living under house arrest in Rome when he wrote a letter of encouragement to the Philippians. Even in prison, heading towards the end of his life, he was incredibly intentional about fulfilling the call of God. He emphasised the need to keep pressing on towards the goal and to finish well what he started. When you have a strong sense of purpose, it's important to identify your goal.

Personal goals can help create motivation and keep momentum. Writing down your goals makes your sense of calling tangible, your dreams more practical and helps you see God's faithfulness when they come to pass.

But how do you know whether your soul goal is something selfish or something spiritual?

In 2017, I remember going through a period of soul searching. It was at a time when I had become so busy with helping others that I had lost a bit of focus on where I was heading. My soul needed a holiday. I spent some time alone with God and wrote down some of the dreams, which I felt were some God-given goals in my journal. I was excited to share them with Steve and was expecting some encouraging feedback. To my disappointment (and this isn't like him), he suggested that my goals were too focussed on myself and my own desires rather than God's.

A time of unusually "intense fellowship" ensued. I felt like he misinterpreted and misunderstood my intentions. I remember heading out for a walk along the spectacular Noosa National Park and poured out my heart to God. I asked God to re-examine my motives, just to make sure I hadn't missed it. I stopped at a café by the water front and pulled out my Bible from my rucksack. The scripture reading for that day was: "May He grant you YOUR heart's desire and fulfil all YOUR plans" (Psalm 20:4 NIV, emphasis added). I felt so relieved. God wants to grant our hearts' desires and plans.

Of course, I happily shared this with Steve on my return. Together, we decided to trust God to give us our hearts' desires and fulfil all our plans. But we also decided to write some specific goals.

When we connect our hearts to God's heart, His desires become our desires.

I am believing that you will combine your desires with His desires. There are so many desires in the heart of God for your calling and purpose. When He sees that your heart aligns with His desires, then He will fulfil them through you. They will succeed.

Recently, I looked back over my journals and saw these entries. It's so obvious to see the faithfulness of God in bringing so many of these goals and dreams to pass. God often instructed the children of Israel to make pillars, monuments, altars and annual festivals as reminders of God's faithfulness in fulfilling His purposes. As New Testament believers, He writes them on our hearts and lives, but we often forget unless we specifically write them down.

When your soul sets God-defined goals, you are set to succeed. Write them down helps you define the goal posts and look back to see God's faithfulness. It will keep your soul recharged.

Your soul needs a goal.

TODAY:

1. Write down three goals, which will help you pursue your calling and the dreams that are in your heart. Keep them in front of you. Look at them regularly. When we keep the goal in front of our eyes, it's easier to believe God will fulfil it.

....

....

2. Share your goals with a spouse or trusted friend/mentor so that they can keep you accountable as you pursue them.

PRAYER:

Lord, I choose to make you my soul's focus today and my sole focus. You are my one thing. I humbly submit my goals and my desires to you. Help me to keep my motives pure. May my desires reflect the desires you have for my life. I press onwards and upwards to follow your path and calling. In Jesus' name, amen.

DAY 25. WHEN YOUR SOUL NEEDS DIRECTION

A man's heart plans his way, But the LORD directs his steps.

PROVERBS 16:9 NKJV

Are you currently navigating a season of change?

Life is all about seasons – most of us go through multiple seasons of transitioning from one stage of life to another. Becoming a student, entering working life, marriage, family, empty nesters, grandkids, locations, and accepting new opportunities. We can often feel anxiety when we go through change.

We often confuse change and transition; they are different.

Change happens to us; transition happens in us.

Change is external; transition is internal.

Transitioning well starts internally, in your soul. Transition is a process that takes time, wisdom and skill.

I have discovered the following four steps are helpful when navigating seasons of transition. I call them "The Four C's of a New Season."

Clarity
When you are in transition there are often many voices speaking to you at the same time. It is important that you tune in to the right voice. Today's verse says it's the Lord that directs your steps. You need to tune in to Him. It is rare that God speaks to you audibly. Usually, He gives clarity in your soul.

Therefore, it's essential that you turn down the volume on distraction and other people's opinions. Take time out of your daily routine. Go somewhere with your Bible and pen and specifically ask God to speak to you soul through prayer, reflection and His Word. Don't overthink it. Don't succumb to the paralysis of analysis.

Instead of over-thinking, try over-thanking!

Thank Him for giving you clarity for your next steps – that your life is in His hands.

Confirmation

If you're anything like me, you'll need lots of confirmations and convincing. "Is this just me or is it God?" God is so kind to us in that He knows we need it, especially when we lack confidence or patience in His timing. He delights in confirming His Word if we are patient to hear Him (see Isaiah 44:24).

Keep your spiritual antennae up and ask Him to speak though His Word, worship, signs, people or situations. Believe that you will see things in His Word you didn't see before. This is the time to ask for guidance from trusted spiritual leaders. Once you have done this, give it time! When we left Australia to return to the UK, it was a huge decision. It took us two years of thinking, praying and processing before we finally moved.

Pastor Bobbie Houston once taught that "everything comes with time, distance, patience, seasons, devotion, commitment, conviction, endurance, steadfastness and the fruit of the spirit. Longevity is carved as you commit to life and calling with others."

Conviction

Conviction is the inner certainty, the resolve and the faith to step out and step into what you believe. Your level of conviction reflects your personal and spiritual maturity.

So let those [of us] who are spiritually mature and full-grown have this mind and hold these convictions; and if in any respect you have a different attitude of mind, God will make that clear to you also.

PHILIPPIANS 3:15 AMPC, EMPHASIS ADDED

An internal conviction is the assurance that it's the right step. When you have a conviction, you believe that you are doing the right thing before God, and you will have confidence in articulating it.

Proverbs 11:3 refers to integrity being a guide for the upright. The word "integrity" comes from the mathematical term for integer. An integer is something that cannot be divided. It is whole and true. Integrity is being true on the outside to what is going on in your soul. When you are doing what you believe God wants you to do, no one can talk you out of it. When you have a conviction, it helps you take decisive action and tell people.

Many older people tell me that that they did not take enough risks in life. They never stepped out on their convictions.

Courage

You need courage to act on your convictions. The courage to step out and the courage to wait for the right time.

Courage is a door handle on the inside. No one else can open it for you. You choose to turn that handle. Courage is not choosing to walk on the familiar ground or the popular path. It's listening to the still small voice and stepping out. Courage is not the absence of fear or failure, it's being scared and doing it anyway.

Get ready to step out, and take a risk. Choose to have that conversation that could change your situation, send that email, start that course, move to that place, start or end that relationship. Enjoy the journey! Don't be so intense! Commit to LOVING every season.

TODAY:

1. Find a quiet spot. Take your Bible and pen. Clear your heart and mind, tune out distractions. Ask God for **clarity** and to **confirm** it through His Word. Write down what you feel He is saying. Choose to get your spiritual antennae up by opening your mind and soul to God's direction. Sometimes this is a process, which can take months. Do not rush the process.

....

....

2. Share your heart with a godly friend or pastor. Continue to look out for signs of **confirmation.**

3. When you believe you have received **confirmation,** make sure it is a **conviction.** This is the time to have **courage** and act.

PRAYER:

Lord, I ask that you would give me clear direction for the next season of my life. Please bring clarity to my heart to plan my way. I thank you that your Word says you will direct my steps. Give me the courage I need to act and to stay in the centre of your will for my life. In Jesus' name, amen.

DAY 26. WHEN YOUR SOUL NEEDS HOPE

Why are you cast down, O my soul? And why are you disquieted within me? Hope in God, for I shall yet praise Him For the help of His countenance.

PSALM 42:5 NKJV

Are you feeling discouraged? Do you need some hope?

You may even be experiencing some "disquieting" of your soul this week. Perhaps someone or something has caused you to feel "cast down" and you feel like giving up. As you pursue the dreams and goals you have identified during *Soul Time*, there will inevitably be opportunities to feel discouraged. That's just life!

Delayed dreams and disappointments can literally make your soul "sick" (see Proverbs 13:12). The Passion Translation puts it this way: "When hope's dream seems to drag on and on, the delay can be depressing. But when at last your dream comes true, life's sweetness will satisfy your soul."

Dreams delayed can drag on and lead to depression. A situation changes, an unfair comment is made, hurtful words are spoken, a disappointing phone call is received, a negative diagnosis is given... There are so many ways that life can knock the wind out of our sails. I call these things Soul Suckers.

I found myself dealing with some Soul Suckers just a few weeks before Colour Conference 2018 in Sydney. Ironically, the theme that year was "Found with wind in her sails." For me, it felt like the wind had gone from my sails! Someone I respected and admired had spoken some words over my life indirectly, and I had allowed them to affect my soul.

Words have an incredible impact on the wellbeing of our soul. We've all been on the receiving end of hurtful words – doesn't it make you feel awful? Hurtful words are Soul Suckers because they attach onto us like a leech and suck the life out of us. The problem with a leech is that if you don't deal with them, they can literally enter the body internally and cause unpleasant health problems! You really don't want that! Don't internalise negative, soul sucking words.

Once the Soul Suckers got into my soul, it massively affected the way I saw myself. I kept smiling, but on the inside, my soul was "disquieted" and "cast down."

Thankfully, during the Colour Conference, God started to speak clearly to me through a powerful and challenging message. He helped me to rise up, brush off the Soul Suckers and speak life-giving words over myself. I praised God with thousands of other women, and at the end of that evening, my soul felt free again.

The next day, I had a good lunch catch-up with my mentor, Margaret Stunt, who helped breathe more fresh wind and perspective into the sails of my soul.

Maybe you are thinking how nice it must be to have a friend like Margaret. But sometimes, we don't have those people around us. It's just ourselves and God! In these situations, we must learn to continually speak truth over our own souls. When your soul needs a holiday, take time to pause, take yourself out for a walk and give yourself a good talking to! Spend more time speaking truth to yourself than listening to yourself!

___

Your external circumstances are only as powerful as your internal securities allow them to be.

___

When you start to speak truth over your soul and silence the Soul Suckers, God's Word gives birth to hope. You can have internal hope even during challenging external circumstances. The last words of Psalm 42 and the last words of Psalm 43 are identical to today's verse. The repetition makes a clear point: May you continue to speak words of hope over your soul today, and every day, as you pursue all that God has for you!

TODAY:

1. What soul sucking words have been spoken over your life? Name them and shame them. Naming is disarming. Decide to stop allowing them to play on repeat in the playlist of your mind.

....

....

2. Remember that as you continually change the words that are speaking, and speak God's Word over your soul, it will change the trajectory of your life. What words will you choose to speak over your soul today?

....

....

PRAYER:

Lord, you know more than anyone how I can get discouraged. Right now, I give every disappointment or negative word spoken over me to you. I choose to praise you, thank you, magnify and exalt you for who you are, for all you've done for me and all you are yet to do. I thank you that I will begin to see the fulfilment of my dreams and experience a sweetness that will satisfy my soul. Help me to speak hope into my soul. In Jesus' name, amen.

DAY 27. WHEN YOUR SOUL DOUBTS GOD'S TIMING

My soul, wait silently for God alone,
For my expectation is from Him.

PSALM 62:5 NKJV

Have you ever doubted God's timing in your life?

Maybe you've prayed for something that hasn't happened as quickly as you expected. As a result, you feel discouraged and disappointed. Throughout *Soul Time,* we have considered your calling, your dreams and your goals. It's also important to consider God's timing.

August 2018 was a huge transition season for us when we returned to England from Australia. We had spent 15 years in Australia and loved being a part of Hillsong Church. Leaving so many people we loved was a real step of faith for us financially. Our daughter, Melody, chose to remain and complete her studies in Brisbane (this a decision we supported, but we weren't expecting COVID-19 to hit and to not be able to see her for 18 months). When we initially returned to England, our housing situation didn't work out and my much-loved Grandma died. It wasn't a great start in many ways.

We met with Pastor Jon Norman feeling a little discouraged. He said something, which really helped us:

"Have a high expectation of God and a low expectation of man."

When we put a high expectation on people, we will often be disappointed. It can cause our soul to doubt God and question His timing. Psalm 62:5 says our soul's expectation needs to come from God alone.

Where are you currently basing your expectation? How much is on people and how much is on God?

David lived with a strong expectation of God and learned to trust God's timing. As a teenager, he was picked out from an identity parade by the prophet Jesse and prophetically anointed to be king (1 Samuel 16). God had already rejected Saul as king (Samuel 15). Everything was looking good when David slayed Goliath and demonstrated all the necessary qualities of a great leader (1 Samuel 17). It seems like only a matter of time before David becomes king. But this "matter of time" was not a few weeks or even months; it would be 17 long and painful years before David became king!

The time between God's promise to David and its fulfilment was 17 years of "between time." "Between time" is the time between God's anointing to David's appointing.

During this time, Saul tries on multiple occasions to kill David. How many times must David have wondered whether he would ever be king. David knew he was anointed, but as the king's spears hurtled towards him, it must have felt like it was never going to happen. But through this process, David's character deepened. He learned to trust God AND trust His timing (see Psalm 31:14). David often declared, "You are my God." In the gap between God's anointing and appointing, you must keep declaring this over your life. When you do this, you are effectively saying, "I trust you! I trust your timing!"

God is not always in a hurry like us! This is difficult to get your head around if you're a get-it-done kind of girl! One passage of scripture, which helps us live in the tension of "between times" is Habakkuk 2:3-4 NKJV:

For the vision is yet for an appointed time; But at the end it will speak, and it will not lie. Though it tarries, wait for it; because it will surely come, it will not tarry. "Behold the proud, His soul is not upright in him; But the just shall live by his faith.

The vision is certain, but often the timing is uncertain. The vision is for an **appointed** time. It tarries, and we must wait for it. The word "tarry" means to wait longer than you expect. But it will surely come!

Do you feel the tension of timing and tarrying in this text? Do you feel this in your own life?

When timing is uncertain and tarrying is required, we are vulnerable to attack from frustration and fear. It's in these times we must trust God's faithfulness and His vision for our future. We place our faith in the faithfulness of God. If you are living "between times," the key is to live by faith because your times are in His hands!

TODAY:

1. Write down a list of things for which you are currently believing God. Even though you are "between times," choose to trust His timing. Don't be discouraged. Choose to stay in faith! Write below your list, "God I trust your timing; my expectation comes from you."

....

....

2. Every time you look at the clock or open your calendar today, declare that your times are in His hands.

PRAYER:

Lord Jesus, I place each of these things I've written down into your hands. By faith, I trust you, and I trust your timing. I keep my expectation high and firmly placed in you. I thank you that every detail of my life is woven together into your perfect plan. I ask this in the name of the Lord Jesus Christ, amen.

DAY 28.
WHEN YOUR
SOUL NEEDS
COURAGE

Love Melody xox

"Have I not commanded you? Be strong and courageous. Do not be terrified; do not be discouraged, for the Lord your God will be with you wherever you go."

JOSHUA 1:9 NIV

Have you ever been fearful? Or maybe you lack courage to step into something God has called you to do?

Every one of us have felt fear at some point in our lives.

Joshua must have felt fear as he took over the huge responsibility from Moses of leading over two million Jews to the promised land. God re-assured him to be strong and not discouraged; He would be with him wherever he went!

Is your soul feeling discouraged?

I have found that it is how we choose to react to fear that determines whether we have courage or become discouraged. Luke's account of Jesus calming the raging storm demonstrates the possibility of finding peace, even when faced with natural fear (see Luke 8:22-25). In the mo-ment of turmoil, the disciples wake Jesus up, warning Him about the storm that threatens to drown them. It's interesting that the disciples don't ask Jesus for help. Instead, they complain about the situation. Fear causes them to fall into discouragement. They forgot they are with the One who cast out demons, raised the dead and healed the sick before their very eyes. He's right there with them, on board the same boat.

Jesus rebukes the bellowing storm and it's calmed in an instant. After this, Jesus says some of the most convicting words in all of scripture: "Why are you fearful? Have you lost your faith in me?" (see Luke 8:25).

Perhaps we find ourselves in these situations more often than we like to ad-mit. We become fearful, stressed and anxious about situations because we focus on the size of the problem facing us rather than the size of the One who lives within us. We are just like the disciples. We are so focused on the chaos that we complain about the situation. We even yell out to Jesus, "We're sink-ing! We're sinking!" But we may never actually take a moment to remember that a miracle-working Jesus is right there within the boat of our own soul.

Think about a time in which you have been afraid. If Jesus asked you why you were fearful – why you didn't have faith in Him – what would you say?

It took courage for me to overcome fear as a young girl when I couldn't sleep at night. My parents bought me a book, *Battlefield of the Mind for Kids* by Joyce Meyer, which taught me to focus on God's Word to overcome the things that appeared so huge in my mind. It took courage for me to discontinue some of the friendships that weren't helping me in my Christian walk in my earlier years at school.

Courage is not walking on familiar ground or the path of least resistance. Courage is not the absence of fear or failure. Courage means stepping out and doing it anyway.

I had to do this many times as I stepped onto a platform to sing as a kid, teen and now as a young adult. It has taken courage to continue living here in Brisbane over the past couple of years when my family moved back to England.

Billy Graham once said, "Courage is contagious." Being around courageous people inspires me. I hope that what I have shared today will put some courage in you! Be encouraged! Have the courage for your convictions. You've got this! God's got you!

TODAY:

The best way to help your soul have courage in a time of fear is to:

1. Remember that no matter what storm you're faced with, Jesus is in your boat. When you are in a storm, play great worship songs that remind you that that Jesus really is with you. For example, listen to Good Grace by Hillsong Music. You can search for it online.

2. Make a whole playlist of songs that can encourage you whenever you go through a storm.

PRAYER:

Lord, I pray that your Spirit would give me the strength to persevere in the face of fear. Thank you that your Word has promised to give me strength and courage. You will never leave me. I declare that fear has no hold over my life, and I'm thankful that you will never leave me. In Jesus' name, amen.

DAY 29.
WHEN YOUR SOUL NEEDS CONFIDENCE

Love Melody xox

Beloved, if our heart does not condemn us, we have confidence toward God.

1 JOHN 3:21 NKJV

Have you ever felt like you weren't capable enough to achieve your God-given destiny?

As a young girl growing up, there have been many factors that have affected my confidence. Living in a world consumed with image, wealth and status, it is easy to let your confidence slip out of your control. Even growing up within a loving family and inside a great church, you can easily lack confidence.

Recently, I watched a talented high school girl doubt her God-given ability to lead worship. She was afraid she couldn't lead others into the presence of God because of who she was and where she came from. How often do we shrink back from God-given opportunities? Godly confidence empowers us to step into them!

This reminded me of the very first time I set foot on a church platform to sing as a fourteen-year-old. It was one Friday night, in a packed auditorium at Hillsong Brisbane. Cass Langton, the creative pastor, come across to the front row towards the end of the service where I was standing with my parents. She asked me if I wanted to lead the praise song at the end and encouraged me, there and then, to jump up! I didn't think I could ever be good enough to lead people in worship. I looked out across the auditorium and there were around 1500 people, which was intimidating. In that moment, I didn't have too much time to overthink my inadequacies, and I just did it. I'm so glad I did. I will always be thankful for Cass and many others since, who believed in me and encouraged me. They helped give me the confidence to step up when I could so easily have stepped back.

Since then, I have found we can be our own worst enemy when it comes to confidence. Sometimes, we can condemn ourselves by doubting who we are and what we are called to do. I have doubted my calling, questioned my abilities and limited my dreams many times since that night. The reality is that I am the only one who can ensure my heart doesn't condemn me or try to put me down. Nobody else can do it for us.

When condemnation creeps into our heart, it can cripple our confidence in God. When our security and identity is rooted in ourselves, in our talent and even in others, we are at risk of misplacing our confidence.

If we are to achieve God's will for our lives, He is the only person in whom we can place our confidence.

Recently, I had the opportunity to encourage a young girl who had allowed her own soul to condemn her. She was constantly pulling herself down. As leaders, we can encourage and inspire people to place their confidence in the One who created and gifted them in the first place. Because I was believed in, I absolutely love helping others to trust God for themselves and step forward with confidence.

So now the case is closed. There remains no accusing voice of condemnation against those who are joined in life-union with Jesus the anointed one.
ROMANS 8:1 TPT

Accusing voices that condemn us are the enemy of confidence. These accusing voices can be other peoples, the enemy and the voice of our own internal critic. The key to overcoming these accusing voices lies in our life-union with Christ.

When we are living in close relationship with Jesus, He becomes the source of our confidence. Jesus is the anointed One, and He anoints us for His purpose in our lives.

I love that this verse begins with "the case is closed." The picture is of a law court where the accusing lawyer has thrown everything he can to condemn you. However, God the Father has listened to everything that has been said and has made the final decision. He decided to throw out the case. It's over!

You no longer need to listen to the accuser! You are who Jesus says you are! You can do what He says you can do!

Replace the condemning lies of the enemy with the Word of God over your life. When you declare His Word over your life, it builds a healthy godly confidence, and this empowers you to step into your future.

TODAY:

1. In what areas has your heart "condemned" you?

....

....

2. Write out three scriptures that you can confess whenever you lack confidence. Write them down and post them around the house. The more you declare these verses, the more you will develop a godly confidence.

....

....

PRAYER:

Dear Lord, help my soul to remember that you are my Good Father and that I have been created in your image. I thank you that I am joined in life-union with you Jesus, and I know that I truly can do all things through your strength. Please remind me when I am weak that you are strong. Help me from the core of my being to declare that my confidence is in you so that I may impact the world around me. Amen.

DAY 30: WHEN YOUR SOUL NEEDS CONFIDENCE

Therefore do not cast away your confidence, which has great reward. For you have need of endurance, so that after you have done the will of God, you may receive the promise:

HEBREWS 10:35-36 NKJV

How often have you thrown away your confidence because of a perceived failure or a somewhat distorted view of how others see you? Maybe you second guess yourself when stepping outside of your comfort zone?

When you throw away your confidence you may also throw away potential opportunities.

After a year as students at Hillsong International Leadership college in Sydney, we were asked to come on staff with the Hillsong team at the Hills Campus. It was a huge honour to be asked. Even though our pastors believed in us, I massively lacked confidence.

I made the mistake of comparing myself to other incredible female leaders on staff that seemed to easily manage the juggle of marriage, family life and leadership.

As female pastors, we helped to host Sisterhood every Thursday morning. I'll never forget one of my very first Sisterhood services. It was a hot summer morning and I was ten weeks pregnant with our second daughter. I had skipped breakfast and was feeling particularly sick. I sat on the front row with the other female pastors, and Pastor Bobbie was reading a graphic excerpt from a book about the barbaric practice of female genital mutilation. I could feel my head start to spin. To my horror, I completely fainted! I literally passed out across Donna Crouch's knee, and she told me afterwards that I was snorting! I had to be carried out of the auditorium with everyone looking on!

When I came around, I was mortified (I did make it into Pastor Bobbie's *Sisterhood* book, which now carries a warning that her message is not for the faint hearted!). Eventually, we all saw the funny side and my colleagues were incredibly supportive. Although I laugh about it now, it shook my confidence at that time.

So many things have the potential to cause us to cast away our confidence. Comparison and being overly concerned about what others think of us are huge confidence killers. Others include external change, a new job, a new baby, moving to a new location, negative words, failure, intimidation... just to name a few!

This scripture in Hebrews encourages us not to throw away our own confidence. If we can throw it away, it demonstrates that we already possess it. Our confidence ultimately comes from who are in Christ and is based on all that He has already done for us.

Therefore, if we throw away our confidence, we have chosen to do this ourselves. We cannot blame a person or a specific situation for our lack of confidence. We have a tendency, particularly as women, to rely on other external factors to help us feel confident. These Confidence Boosters include:

- People's approval
- Our position
- Our successes
- Our health
- A boyfriend or husband
- The level of encouragement we receive
- A specific career or ministry opportunity

All these things can be fantastic. However, we cannot base our confidence on ANY of the above. They are all subject to change and can bring potential disappointment.

In recent years, I've put together a Confidence Kit that can prevent you from throwing away your confidence.

Confidence in your Calling

In Hebrews 10:35-36 confidence relates to doing the will of God. When you know you are fulfilling the call of God, it builds confidence and recharges your soul.

"Now then, it is through my union with Jesus Christ, that I enjoy an enthusiasm and confidence in my ministry for God."

ROMANS 15:17 TPT

Confidence in your Creator

Our confidence MUST be in the God who made us in His image, with unique abilities, personality and gifting.

We are God's masterpiece. He has created us anew in Christ Jesus, so we can do the good things he planned for us long ago.

EPHESIANS 2:10 NLT

Confidence in Crisis

Crisis can cause us to shrink back and retreat for self-preservation. We can try to cover this up by working harder and avoiding confrontation and rejection.

...God is your confidence in times of crisis, keeping your heart at rest in every situation.

PROVERBS 3:26 TPT

Confidence in His Completion

God is the One who completes, promotes, provides and fulfils His promise over your life.

*...being **confident** of this very thing, that He who has begun a good work in you will COMPLETE it until the day of Jesus Christ."*
PHILIPPIANS 1:6 NKJV, EMPHASIS ADDED

American actress and entrepreneur, Blake Lively, once said, "The most beautiful thing you can wear is confidence."

Don't throw away your godly confidence; wear it with authority!

TODAY:

1. What Confidence Killers cause you to throw away your confidence? If you can identify these triggers, you can guard against them.

2. Can you identify your Confidence Boosters? Remind yourself not to rely on them.

PRAYER:

Lord Jesus, help me to base my confidence firmly in you. Help me to ensure you are the foundation and the cornerstone of my confidence. Help me not to misplace my confidence or throw it away. May I wear confidence with humility and authority as I step forward into all that you have for me. In Jesus' name, amen.

DELVE DEEPER

I pray that as you've read and responded to this daily devotional that your soul is feeling rested, replenished and recharged again! I hope that as you've actioned the daily *Soul Time* suggestions, you will have found a fresh love and healthy respect for the wellbeing of your soul. The benefits have perhaps left you desiring more, like the benefits of a good holiday when you just want it to last longer!

This section is for your "extended holiday" – a chance to delve a little deeper into the gold of God's Word, reflect a little longer and perhaps share a little heart-to-heart with a trusted friend, mentor or small group.

Like the daily devotional, you will receive some practical responses to help guide you further in applying God's Word to your life. Keep your journal and pen beside you as you read and reflect – jot down scriptures, ideas and heartfelt prayers.

I love being on this journey with you and count it such a privilege to speak into your life during this season. My prayer is that your *Soul Time* will go to a new level of intimacy and vulnerability with God, yourself and others.

Much love,
Rachel

DAY 1:
WHEN YOUR SOUL NEEDS TO BE HEALTHY

DELVE

A healthy soul starts with an understanding of what it means to be His BELOVED. It means you are loved unconditionally without having to earn His love. Have you subconsciously been trying to earn God's love through what you do for God or others?

Read the following verses, which affirm that you are His beloved:

– Romans 1:7
– Romans 9:25
– 1 Corinthians 15:58
– Colossians 3:12

DEEPER

Listen to what God is saying to you through these verses and write down your responses to these questions:

Right from the beginning of this soul holiday, what areas of your life need to move forwards or become healthier?

....

....

How can you do this from a position of internal rest rather than trying to earn His love?

....

....

DAY 2:
WHEN YOUR SOUL NEEDS TO FEEL WHOLE

DELVE

In this time of rest, surrender again all that you are to the One who created you and makes you complete. Meditate on these scriptures so your whole body, soul and spirit can rest in Him, follow Him and bring Him praise:

– Psalm 63:5, 8
– Psalm 103:1

DEEPER

We may know we are whole, but in order to live it out, we need to declare we are whole! Using the truth of God's Word, compose a short declaration that you can speak out loud each morning.

(You may wish to start with "I am complete in Him....")

....

....

DAY 3:
WHEN YOUR SOUL FEELS CLUTTERED

DELVE

– Read Luke 6: 43-45

Jesus had just been teaching His disciples on how to love, how to forgive, how to give and how to keep your own motives right. He then asserts that the treasure in your heart will be evident in your life. As God speaks to you through this passage, think about what you need to get rid of and about the treasure God has placed in your heart. Thank God for it.

DEEPER

Decide how you will declutter. Perhaps you will commit to regular walks where you can think clearly; you may need to reduce your social media intake; or examine the people you spend the most time with and how they impact your soul.

List below some external habits you can change to keep your soul healthy:

1. ....

2. ....

3. ....

DAY 4:
WHEN YOUR SOUL FEELS FLAT

DELVE

Often, things in life can be so familiar to us that we forget to delve deeper. This psalm is well known to many but will lift your soul as you take time to really think about the power and meaning of the declarations.

– Read Psalm 118

Firstly, look at all the verses, which refer to the opposition David faces and notice how he responds.

Secondly, check out the verses where David makes faith-filled declarations. Discuss these in a group or with a mentor/friend.

DEEPER

Create your own faith-filled declarations, write them down and speak them daily over your life.

Faith-filled Declarations

....

....

DAY 5:
WHEN YOUR SOUL IS FRETTING

DELVE

Be still for five minutes, turn off your phone and tune out all distractions.

– Memorise and meditate on Isaiah 30:15

Note down what the Lord is saying in the quiet:

....

....

DEEPER

– Read Isaiah 30:18-26

This passage is full of God's gracious promises to His battle-weary people. It lists several promises to those who place their confidence in Him.

Choose a promise to speak over yourself each morning and night.

God's Promise for Me

....

....

DAY 6:
WHEN YOUR SOUL IS DISTRESSED

DELVE

Psalm 42 begins with David's soul longing for God. The presence of God is drawn towards souls that are thirsty and invite Him into their space.

Discuss with a like-minded friend how you can increase your awareness of and thirst for God's presence.

DEEPER

– Study Psalm 63

This is a time when David longs to be in the sanctuary in Jerusalem because in the Old Testament, this was where the presence of God was located. David cannot access the sanctuary because he is in the wilderness of Judah, running from those who are trying to kill him. The wilderness speaks of the lonely seasons when God seems far away.

Which verses in Psalm 63 demonstrate David's commitment to press into God despite his external circumstances?

....

....

Take a few extra moments on your soul holiday to purposefully develop the practice of pressing into the presence of God through praise. What are you praising God for today?

....

....

DAY 7:
WHEN YOUR SOUL BATTLES WITH COMPARISON

DELVE

– Read Matthew 25:14-30
– Now focus on verse 15.

Notice that the servants were entrusted according to their ability.

Write down the talents God has entrusted you with, and thank Him for them:

....

....

DEEPER

Now think about how you can strengthen and grow your God-given talents:

– Read verse 19

Sometimes we can wait a long time before our talents are noticed, let alone rewarded.

How can you continue to be faithful with what is in your hand?

....

....

– Read verses 25-29

When you use what you are given without comparison you will be given more!

What talent are you hiding out of fear of what others will think?

....

....

DAY 8:
WHEN YOUR SOUL NEEDS TO FEEL LOVED

DELVE

Reflect on God's love **for you,** and spend some time thanking Him for His love **for you.**

Write out a prayer in response to God's love:

....

....

DEEPER

Have a closer look at these incredible statements:

– Psalm 139:1-3
– Psalm 36:5-6
– Psalm 51:1-2
– Psalm 107:8
– Psalm 42

How do these verses reinforce your soul's understanding of God's love for you and the value He places on you?

....

....

DAY 9:
WHEN YOUR SOUL HAS TRUST ISSUES

DELVE

Make a list of all the things for which you have trusted God in the past where He has been faithful:

1.
....

2.
....

3.
....

Now make a list of all the things for which you are currently trusting God:

1.
....

2.
....

3.
....

Take some soul time to thank God for His faithfulness to you in the past and for His faithfulness for your future.

DEEPER

– Read Psalm 28:7

Now find other scriptures in the Bible that encourage you to trust God. Write them out, and speak them over your list of things for which you are trusting God.

....

....

DAY 10:
WHEN YOUR SOUL NEEDS TO STIR UP CREATIVITY

DELVE

– **Read Psalm 8:1-3**
– **Read Psalm 104:24-30**

What a wildly wonderful world, God!

What can you do creatively to reflect the excellent and diverse nature of our God?

....

....

Save a note in your calendar to remind you to bring fresh creativity to your life, work or ministry.

DEEPER

– **Listen to the worship song, So Will I (Hillsong Music)[9]**

Mediate on how the lyrics emphasise the detail of God's creation, and surrender your own creative ideas to Him again.

---

9   Hillsong Music, written by Joel Houston, Benjamin Hastings, Michael Fatkin.

DAY 11:
WHEN YOUR SOUL NEEDS A SPA

DELVE

– Read Luke 2:52

We can see here that during those 30 unseen years of essential preparation for ministry, Jesus grew strong mentally, physically, spiritually and relationally. If these were the markers of growth in His life as God's Son, how much more do we need them to prepare for what God has in store for our future?

DEEPER

Share your RPM'S "dashboard" with friends or in a group. Look at how you can bring accountability to each other to step up to the next level in a particular area.

Make sure you're intentional about planning your next day off, and ensure it's a day that replenishes your soul. Do at least one thing during the day that impacts each area of your RPM'S "dashboard."

Plan your day:

Morning

....

Afternoon

....

Evening

....

DAY 12:
WHEN YOUR SOUL NEEDS MORE

DELVE

Sometimes, as I described in my story, we can look for other things to satisfy hunger temporarily (i.e., relationships, movies, retail, affirmation, even podcasts).

Think about the things in your life that you may subconsciously hunger for to fulfil your soul, when it's more of God that you really need. Note them down here, and commit them to God:

....

....

DEEPER

– Read John 6:35
– Jesus makes the incredible statement that He is the bread of life.
– Our only place of satisfaction.
– Next, focus on Matthew 5:6

We were created to feel spiritual hunger. In the famous Beatitudes, Jesus spoke about the importance of spiritual hunger and the promise of being filled.

What do you need more of in your life?

....

....

DAY 13:
WHEN YOUR SOUL NEEDS A GOD-ENCOUNTER

DELVE

When you encounter God, you are changed to be more like Him. What happens internally is reflected externally.

Read the following verse. Journal or discuss how your life has changed after a God-encounter moment. How are you becoming more like Jesus?

– 2 Corinthians 3:16-18

....

....

DEEPER

Now focus on the following verse:

– Proverbs 8:17

How can you purposefully seek God in your day-to-day life and look for God-encounter moments?

....

....

Pray with a close friend or two, either at home, in a group or on a prayer walk. Talk about living with a heightened awareness of and need for the presence of God in your lives.

DAY 14:
WHEN YOUR SOUL NEEDS TO ENLARGE

DELVE

– Read the whole of Isaiah 54

It is a very powerful chapter packed with promises; let the words encourage you and enlarge your heart.

DEEPER

Choose the three verses or promises that specifically encourage you. Write them below and what God is saying to you through them. Intentionally declare them over yourself and your family. Share your favourite one with a friend or group.

1. ....

2. ....

3. ....

DAY 15:
WHEN YOUR SOUL NEEDS TO HEAR FROM GOD

DELVE

Fill your environment with worship music today. Meditate on God's promises, begin to pray and declare these verses over yourself as you purposely pursue God:

– Psalm 91:14-15
– Mathew 7:7
– James 4:8
– Matthew 28:20

DEEPER

In Luke 5:16, Jesus models the need to purposefully pursue God by finding a place to be with Him. For Jesus, it was in the wilderness – where is it for you?

Book in time this week to go to your secret place. Allow your soul to hear from God.

What is He saying to you?

....

....

DAY 16:
WHEN YOUR SOUL NEEDS TO LOVE

DELVE

God loves us with *agape* love. What is *agape* love? How would you define it?

Think about how *agape* love differs from some of the conceptions of love that we have in society today.

Study 1 Corinthians 13

The Apostle Paul writes "an *anthem* to agape" here. Which attributes of *agape* love stand out to you the most today?

....

....

DEEPER

– Read John 13:34 and John 14:15

Responding to these verses, discuss the following with a friend, mentor or in a group: How does the Holy Spirit enable us to love?

Identify a person you are struggling to love in your own strength. Then pray the prayer below, and ask the Holy Spirit to fill you with His love for this person.

Heavenly Father, You are the God of love; thank you for loving me. Lord, I choose to love others as you have first loved me. In this moment, I pray that you will fill me afresh by the power of the Holy Spirit so that I can truly love (add person's name). Soften my heart so that I can love them as you do, and help me to demonstrate your love as I actively choose to extend your heart towards them. Thank you that I can do all things in your strength.

IN JESUS' NAME, AMEN.

DAY 17:
WHEN YOUR SOUL NEEDS TO DREAM

DELVE

– Read Acts 2:1-21

Now focus on verses 17-18 where Peter quotes the prophet Joel.
Notice how he connects dreams with:

– the outpouring of the Holy Spirit
– the last days
– building the church

What is this reminding you today about your dreams?

....

....

DEEPER
Write out your dream below:

....

....

Think and pray about your dream:

How can you make sure your dream is from the Holy Spirit?

How can your dream contribute to what God is doing on the earth right
now? How does it help build His kingdom?

DAY 18:
WHEN YOUR SOUL NEEDS REFRESHING FRIENDSHIPS

DELVE

Read the following scriptures on friendship:

– Job 6:14
– Ecclesiastes 4:9-12
– Proverbs 27:17
– Proverbs 17:9
– Proverbs 17:17

Think about the friends in your life and whether their friendship reflects these verses. How do you think people would describe you as a friend?

DEEPER

Our friends can influence our future, encourage us, love us and be there through life's highs and lows. Therefore, we need to be intentional about those friends who are good for our soul.

Write down the names of friends you can become more intentional with after this soul holiday. Plan to encourage and spend time with them.

....

....

DAY 19:
WHEN YOUR SOUL NEEDS TO FLOURISH

DELVE

– Read Psalm 92

I love the analogy of us being like palm trees in verse 12. I saw lots of palm trees while living in Queensland. I love them!

These are the qualities of a palm tree:

– Built to withstand storms, desert climate, tsunamis etc.
– Fruitful
– An oasis and shelter; a place of refreshing
– Known for its attractive blossoms
– Evergreen

The cedars of Lebanon were extremely strong and durable. They were used to build the temple and kings' palaces.

In what ways would you love your soul to be stronger and have these qualities?

....

....

....

....

....

....

DEEPER

– Read verse 14

What beautiful words! Write them out, and mediate on how your life can grow in grace, thrive and bear fruit year after year. Thank God that your soul will be rich in trust, love and contentment.

....

....

....

....

....

....

....

....

DAY 20:
WHEN YOUR SOUL NEEDS A SHOT OF PASSION

DELVE

The Passion Translation (TPT) is a modern, easy-to-read Bible version that aims to alight a fresh delight for Jesus.

Read and study the following scriptures from The Passion Translation:

– **Psalm 63:8**
– **Romans 12:11**
– **Psalm 69:9**
– **Philippians 2:13**

What do these verses teach about alighting a fresh passion in you?

....

....

DEEPER

Think about what <u>you</u> can do to stir up passion. What people do you find helpful in stirring up your passion for God?

What three things will you do in your soul holiday to make sure you are intentional about maintaining, and even increasing, your personal level of passion for God?

1. ....

2. ....

3. ....

DAY 21:
WHEN YOUR SOUL NEEDS ASSURANCE OF YOUR CALLING

DELVE

There are several "call narratives" in the Bible. You may already have a favourite "call narrative" of your own.

Study one or more of these stories, and discover how God calls individuals to fulfil His purpose:

– Moses: see Exodus 3
– Jeremiah: see Jeremiah 1
– Isaiah: see Isaiah 6
– Jonah: see Jonah 1-2

DEEPER

What is the one thing you feel God is speaking to your soul from the "call narratives"?

....

....

Take some time to note down the reasons why YOU are who God has called to make a difference!

....

....

DAY 22:
WHEN YOUR SOUL NEEDS TO DREAM AGAIN

DELVE

Study the story of Joseph and how to dream again:

– Read Genesis 37-50

What do you think were the darkest times in Joseph's life?

....

....

Why did God continue to work in Joseph's life and situation in order to fulfil His God-given dream?

....

....

DEEPER

You have visualised your dreams and jotted them down. As you commit them to God, what is He saying and promising over them?

....

....

It's time to be brave and make some decisions! How will you take a step towards your dream?

....

....

DAY 23:
WHEN YOUR SOUL NEEDS PURPOSE

DELVE

– Read John 18:37

Jesus knew exactly His reason for being on the earth. He was on the earth for a powerful cause. This cause was a deep conviction. His cause kept his mission clear.

A soul holiday is the perfect time to think again about your cause. What is most important to you? What has God called you to?

....

....

DEEPER

Choose one of the following:

– Write your life mission in one sentence

When life gets busy and distractions come thick and fast, ask yourself on a regular basis, "Is this helping me to achieve my purpose?"

– Write The Marriage We See with your spouse

Steve and I went away for a weekend and wrote this document. It was 150 words long and can be printed out onto one page. Once we completed it, we printed it out and placed it in our bedroom. Whenever we do marriage preparation classes, we encourage young couples to do this exercise.

Once a year, we go away and review *The Marriage We See.* We evaluate what we are doing well and what we need to work on. It's not always an easy process, but it has helped us build our marriage by design and not default.

DAY 24:
WHEN YOUR SOUL NEEDS A GOAL

DELVE

Take the time to study Philippians 3:12-16 in more detail.

– Read it several times in a few different versions of the Bible.

Write down all the things that you believe God is saying to you from these verses:

....

....

DEEPER

Find a commentary on Philippians or some notes in a study Bible. If you are an audible learner, try and find a sermon or podcast on this passage.

How did these resources add to your understanding of what it means to "press towards the goal of the upward call in Christ Jesus"?

....

....

DAY 25:
WHEN YOUR SOUL NEEDS DIRECTION

DELVE

Look at another well-known scripture that talks about being led by our heart or soul.

– Proverbs 3:5-6

How easy is it for you to "lean to your own understanding"? Are you an overthinker? Share these tendencies with a mentor or group, and talk about how you can get your antennae up to hear from God more clearly and lean on Him.

DEEPER

Write a list of ten things you are thankful for in this season. It will help reduce the anxiety or pressure around choosing your next step to take.

1. ....

2. ....

3. ....

4. ....

5. ....

6. ....

7. ....

8. ....

9. ....

10. ....

In what area do you need the courage to step out in your convictions? Ask someone to agree with you in prayer that you'll be confident as you step out.

....

DAY 26:
WHEN YOUR SOUL NEEDS HOPE

DELVE

– Study Psalm 42

In the first four verses, the psalmist is discouraged and downcast. What clues can you find in these verses to explain why the psalmist may have been downcast? Can you relate to any of these reasons?

....

DEEPER

In verses 6-11 the psalmist makes some progress to break free of discouragement. How does the psalmist intentionally change his perspective in these verses?

....

....

How can you put these principles into action in your own life in a practical way?

....

....

DAY 27:
WHEN YOUR SOUL DOUBTS GOD'S TIMING

DELVE

Study:

– Psalm 31
– Psalm 62

Read each of these in a couple of different versions. Try and access a commentary if you have one.

DEEPER

Identify the verses or phrases in the two psalms where David encourages you:

1. To focus your expectation on God

....

2. To not place your expectation in man

....

3. To trust God with your heart or soul in the "between times"

....

What verse or phrase spoke to you the most from your study and why?

....

....

DAY 28:
WHEN YOUR SOUL NEEDS COURAGE

DELVE

– Read Psalm 23

Encourage yourself with this well-known psalm today. Remind yourself what it means for Jesus to be your good Shepherd.

What valleys of fear or discouragement are you walking through? Imagine Him walking WITH you through them to the other side. Take some time to thank God in advance for what He is going to do.

Lord, today I am thankful because...

....

....

DEEPER

– Focus on Psalm 23:4

We can walk through a dark valley with a refreshed soul.

Discuss with a friend or group what you do to overcome fear, and encourage each other as you choose to respond to fear by stepping out in courage.

Lord, today I choose courage because...

....

....

DAY 29:
WHEN YOUR SOUL NEEDS CONFIDENCE
(MELODY)

DELVE

Speak this verse over yourself and a current situation in which you don't feel capable:

– Proverbs 3:26

How can you keep your heart and soul at rest when self-accusing thoughts come?

....

....

DEEPER

Plan to spend a little longer today focusing on the awesome nature of your God. Allow your heart to be in awe of Him. Love and confidence will flood your heart leaving little or no room for self-condemnation.

Meditate and pray on this scriptural truth:

– Proverbs 14:26

If you have children, pray that your devotion and confidence will impact their lives and that they will live in security.

Write out a bold statement of how you will walk in confidence and strength today.

....

....

DAY 30:
WHEN YOUR SOUL NEEDS CONFIDENCE
(RACHEL)

DELVE

Here's a reminder of the confidence kit I referred to in the daily devotion. It has helped so many people. I encourage you to make this your own by adding your own scriptures under each heading:

Confidence in your Calling

– Romans 15:17

What scriptures speak to you about calling?

....

....

....

Confidence in your Creator

– Ephesians 2:10

Note down powerful scriptures about your creator:

....

....

....

Confidence in Crisis

– Proverbs 3:26

What other scriptures help you to remain confident in crisis?

....

....

....

Confidence in His Completion

– Philippians 1:6
– Colossians 2:10

God is the One who completes, promotes, provides and fulfils His promise over your life. Study and memorise these two scriptures so you can recall them throughout the day.

DEEPER

Write a list of all the qualities He has invested in you and the gifts and strengths that you bring to the table. This can be a very powerful exercise. If you get stuck, ask some of your closest friends what should be on your list. Keep them on your phone or a place where you can see them regularly. Confidently bring these strengths to every situation you face this week.

....

....

GRATITUDE

The older I get, the more grateful I am to have had the passion and priority for God's House exemplified to me and my children. An intentional personal relationship with the Holy Spirit, and high value placed on putting God first in our lives, have set a firm foundation that has kept our family strong. My Grandad pioneered our church in Norwich 56 years ago, and my parents pastored for 30 years before handing on to our dear friends, Jon and Chantel Norman, in 2014. Their years of faithfulness, their commitment to the cause of Christ and their ability to hand on the baton when it was time with strength and humility are an inspiration to many church leaders. My parent's passion for God's House and excitement for our new building remain consistent as they continue to be our greatest encouragers and prayer warriors.

I will always be grateful for the impact that Brian and Bobbie Houston have had on our lives as our pastors and bosses for 15 years. Our daughters couldn't have been raised in a more empowering environment than that of Hillsong Church Australia. I am so very thankful for the many Hillsong pastor friends along the way, particularly in the early days, such as Donna Crouch and Phil and Lucinda Dooley, who saw potential in us and encouraged us to fulfil our dreams and calling. We will always be thankful for Cassandra Langton for seeing the gold in Melody and for drawing out the calling on her life to lead worship. We dearly love those in Brisbane who have been part of her journey, in particular Brad and Karissa Kohring, for giving her the opportunity to lead worship with confidence and mentoring her along the way.

I am beyond grateful for the time Robert Fergusson invested in both Steve and I to develop our preaching and communication. We seriously learned from the best. He would sit with us over a meal or coffee and download jewels of wisdom around God's Word and the call to preach. His feedback and belief in me were pivotal in helping me find my voice with confidence as a woman. I will forever be grateful. I regularly refer to what he taught me over the years as I coach pastors and leaders now.

A massive thanks to Sheila Vollar, who helped me get my thoughts down in the early stages of this devotional – knowing how much to include and what to cut, when I had journals and journals full of material and a passion to share everything!

Thank you to Katy Cooper for her excellent English skills and her ability to help clarify and structure the "Delve Deeper" section. Thank you to Celina Mina, for her editorial and publishing insights.

Finally, to my darling hubby, Steve Mawston, who gave me much of the inspiration and encouragement to write this devotional. His constant ability to genuinely cheer me on to be all God has called me to be is both releasing and grounding. His exceptional writing, editing, feedback and research skills, as well as his own love for God's Word, unite us in cause and call. After 28 years of marriage, I love him dearly now more than ever, and I know I'm a better leader and communicator because of him.

Ultimately, to Jesus, my Lord, Saviour and best friend. May this bring glory to His name and draw many souls closer to Him.

ABOUT THE AUTHORS

Rachel Mawston has dedicated her life to building the church and people's lives. She is passionate about pursuing the call of God and helping others do the same and see their dreams and potential fulfilled. She was a worship pastor in her home church in Norwich for many years as well as working as a physiotherapist for 15 years. She is married to her teen sweetheart and soul mate, Steve Mawston, and they have two incredible daughters, Melody and Mercy.

Steve and Rachel attended Hillsong International Leadership College in Sydney and had the privilege of serving on Hillsong Church staff in both Sydney and Brisbane as pastors for over 14 years. They returned to their homeland in 2018 where they are loving being based at Soul Church, as part of the Senior Leadership Team with lifelong friends, Pastors Jon and Chantel Norman.

Steve and Rachel are also committed to preaching, teaching and coaching pastors and leaders across the United Kingdom. Rachel is known for bringing faith and passion in a personal, prophetic and practical way when she preaches God's Word. She has the unique ability to love people on and off the platform, inspiring them to walk closer with God and stirring up their dreams and God-given potential.

Rachel has a zest for life that is fun and contagious. She loves the beautiful British countryside, sunshine, beach holidays, power walks, paddle boarding, movies, theme parks, spas, high teas, entertaining and good times enjoyed with good people and good food!

Melody Mawston is like her mum, sharing a passion for God's House and pursuing the call of God. She currently lives in Brisbane and is completing her Bachelor in Theology. She has been passionate about worship since leading worship as a young child in Hillsong Kids. She now has the honour of leading worship at Hillsong Church Brisbane. She is a song writer and is currently working on an album to help people reflect and draw closer to God in challenging seasons.

Melody has an amazing pastoral heart for others and loves empowering them to develop and grow in their potential. She loves all things Disney, travel, spas and is a lover of great food – she loves to entertain and is a great event planner of good times!